the *Book of Bible Prayers*

collected and prayer-a-phrased from God's Word

by

Mary Harwell Sayler

For Bob, our family, our church family,
and all who seek the Lord in prayer

ISBN: 9781692166069
Imprint: Independently published

In the time of Adam and Eve's grandson,
"People began to call on the Name of the Lord,"
Genesis 4:26.

Foreword

This book doesn't talk *about* prayer. It *is* prayer – a book with the actual prayers prayed over the centuries by diverse peoples of God and recorded in the Bible.

Most likely, you've discovered many excellent books *about* prayer as well as prayer books that arose from the liturgy in various churches, but this book crosses denominational lines, giving us over 250 prayers to pray in private or together as one voice, one people of God. In addition, this collection assures anyone praying in solitude of having "prayer partners," not only from other people using the book today but also those who originated the prayer, for, in God, time is irrelevant.

As Bible prayers came together for this book, an issue quickly arose about which translation to use – an important factor since every prayer taken from one translation automatically excludes the others. This could be resolved by going back and forth between different English versions, but the more translations, the more permissions required from publishers, unless, of course, we rely on the beloved *King James Version* (KJV) of the Bible, which is in the public domain.

Like countless people, I'm fond of the poetic KJV, translated from Hebrew, Greek, Aramaic, and Latin manuscripts around the time of Shakespeare when English was in its infancy. Centuries later, the *Revised Standard Version* (RSV) helped to ease comprehension, and when the *Good News Bible* (aka *Today's English Version*) came out, many of us read it again and again with understanding and delight!

As other contemporary versions came into print, millions embraced the *New International Version* (NIV) while I read the *New American Bible* (NAB), *New American Standard Bible* (NASB), *New Jerusalem Bible* (NJV), *New English Bible* (NEB), *Revised English Bible* (REB), *Amplified Bible* (AB), *New Revised*

Standard Version (NRSV), *New King James Version* (NKJV), *New Living Translation* (NLT), *New American Bible, Revised Edition* (NABRE), the *Message,* the *Voice,* the *Common English Bible* (CEB), *English Standard Version* (ESV), the *Holman Christian Standard Bible* (HCSB), the *Christian Standard Bible* (CSB), and a translation ideally entitled, *God's Word.*

I just wanted to find my own favorite version! Almost everyone I knew had one, but that has never happened for me, and now, I love them all! I value the unique choices of synonyms, syntax, and phrases that translators have made in an effort to be both accurate and clear in word and meaning.

The results revealed the same biblical truths freshly expressed, helping us to see what we might not notice otherwise. And so, in thinking about the present book, I felt urged to revisit the major translations from my bookshelves and the Bible Gateway website before prayerfully paraphrasing the prayers into words we might use in everyday conversation.

Once the idea of "prayer-a-phrasing" Bible prayers took hold, I saw that all prayers are not created equal! Some were meant for a specific time, place, situation, or person, such as praying for a sign of confirmation or asking if God wanted the people to go into battle. Some repeated previous prayers, while others went on and on unless edited or divided into shorter prayers as occasionally done here. Still other Bible prayers called down disasters we wouldn't wish on anyone this side of the cross! If, though, a "negative" prayer still relates to present-day lives, it has most likely been included. However, I purposely omitted allusions to prayer and, regretfully, had to leave out most of the wonderful poetry of Isaiah, who primarily spoke *for* God, rather than *to* Him. Hopefully, though, actual prayers relevant to today have not been excluded – at least not intentionally!

Regardless of the likely imperfections in my work, the prayers in these pages can help us to connect with God and identify more strongly with God's people from ancient days to the present. As we see how real Bible people of faith prayed, their prayers can broaden our views of praying and of getting honest with God.

But, you might ask, don't we already have a Bible prayer book? If you love the Psalms, as I do, you have surely discovered its effective prayers or heard of its use as a prayer book by Jesus and our Judeo-Christian family for centuries. You may have noticed, too, that most of those 150 poetic writings can be categorized as songs, praise, thanksgiving, statements of faith, complaints, or laments – each of which makes a wonderful prayer-starter or daily devotional. However, less than half the psalms record actual prayers, which, Lord willing, have been prayerfully paraphrased into contemporary language here.

Those prayer-a-phrased psalms fall about midway in the book as happens with Psalms in The Book, too, which isn't surprising as these pages follow the Genesis-to-Revelation order with which we're most familiar. Some might wish the prayers had been grouped according to topics such as prayers of faith, lament, thanks, or cries for comfort, but determining each subject is, well, subjective. To ease your search, however, the straight-through-the-Bible order of the prayers should help. Also, you will find an index in the back of the book with page numbers alongside the alphabetized names of the one(s) who prayed as well as a brief, identifying fact about each person.

By following the traditional arrangement of the biblical books, I discovered something I hadn't expected. i.e., The prayers in the Hebrew scriptures (aka "Old Testament") are frequently pleas, praise, thanksgiving, complaints, or petitions, but in the New Testament such requests or responses are less likely to occur. Instead, Paul and other apostles typically ask believers in Christ to pray for them. Or, more often, they offer parental blessings over the Christian communities they're addressing. Similar to the priestly blessing of Aaron in Numbers 6, these New Testament blessings are directed toward the people rather than

God, but I felt I would be remiss to exclude all of them, so a few of those blessings have been prayer-a-phrased as prayers. Or, in the case of Melchizedek, his words remain as a well-placed blessing, appropriately beginning this book.

Although every book of the Bible is not represented, two versions of the powerful prayer of Jesus in the "Our Father/ Lord's Prayer" have been included. You'll also find His "High Priestly Prayer" from John 17 to further empower these pages and enrich a prayer book we can pick up, take with us, and turn to whenever we need a "prayer partner" or want words to speak for us when we have trouble expressing ourselves.

Whether prayers are presented in archaic words, contemporary language, or something in between, God's Word is alive and lively! And so, I pray these timeless prayers from the Bible will expand our prayer-vision, unite us as God's people, strengthen our faith, and deepen our devotion to God as we pray for our families, our churches, our communities, our country, our world, and ourselves.

May God bless you and your prayer life in the Lord.

Mary Harwell Sayler
www.bibleprayers.net

Prayers from the Torah, Psalms, and Prophets

Genesis 14:19-20 – the blessing of Melchizedek

May you be blessed by God most High,
maker of heaven and earth.

May you be blessed by God most High,
Who has delivered you from the hands
of those who wish you harm.

Genesis 15:2 – a prayer of Abraham

O Lord God, what will You give me?

*Will I need an inheritance
if I have no child?*

Genesis 16:13 – a prayer of Hagar

You are EL Roi!
You are the God Who sees me!
You watch over me.

Genesis 17:18 – a prayer of Abraham

*Oh, that my child
might live in Your
presence, Lord,
and be under Your
blessing!*

Genesis 18:23, 32 – a prayer of Abraham

Lord, would You really sweep away
the righteous with the wicked?

What if ten honorable people
are found?

And God answered:

For the sake of ten,
I will not destroy the town.

Genesis 21:6 – a prayer of Sarah

*God, You have given me
joyous laughter!*

*Everyone who hears of this
will laugh with me.*

Genesis 24:12 – a prayer of Abraham's servant

Oh, Lord
God of my master,
please grant me
success today
and show me
Your steadfast
love!

Genesis 25:21-22 – a prayer of Rebekah

Why, God?

*Why is this
happening*

to me?

Genesis 28:20-22 – a prayer of Jacob

Lord God, if You will be with me
   and
watch over me wherever I go
   and
provide me with necessities
   and
get me safely home,
   then
You will be my God.

Genesis 32:10-11 – a prayer of Jacob

*Lord, I am not worthy
of all the loving kindness
and faithfulness
You have shown me,
for I began with nothing
and now have far more
than I could ever need.*

*But, Lord, I'm alarmed
by those I fear might
harm me and my family.
Please deliver us, I pray.*

Genesis 32:26 – a prayer of Jacob

Lord, I will
not let
You go
until
You bless me!

Genesis 48:15-16 – a prayer of Jacob

God, You have walked with my family
and tended me all my life and sent
Your angel to protect me from evil.

>*Bless these my children.*

Let my name – our family name
>*be honored in them.*

Let them fill the earth.

Exodus 3:4 – a prayer of Moses

Here I am, Lord

Exodus 4:13

O Lord, send someone else!

Exodus 5:21-22 – a prayer of Moses

*Lord, why
have You brought
so much trouble
on Your people?*

Why did You send me?

*Ever since I got here
things have gotten worse,
and You've done nothing
to help!*

Exodus 15:6, 11, 13, 17-18 – a prayer of Moses

How glorious and powerful is Your hand, O Lord!
Your right hand holds back the enemy.

No god among them is like You, Lord,
for You alone are gloriously pure,
praise-worthy, and able to perform wonders.

You guide Your people whom You have
redeemed by Your faithful love;
With strength, You lead us to holy places.

You bring us to the land You possess
and settle us in the place You prepared
for us to dwell.

Lord, Your hands create a sanctuary,
and You will reign forever and ever!

Exodus 15:21 – a prayer of Miriam

We sing to You, Lord
for You are to be exalted!

How gloriously You
have triumphed!

Exodus 32:11-13 – a prayer of Moses

*O, Lord, why are You so angry
with Your people – the very ones
You rescued with such great power?*

*After displaying Your mighty force,
do You really want everyone
to think You brought us here
to strike us dead?*

*Please do not bring disaster!
Remember Your faithful servants
who have gone before us –
Abraham, Isaac, Jacob –
and how You promised them
countless descendants
more numerous than stars.*

Exodus 32:31-32 – a prayer of Moses

(Now I see)

what terrible sins
these people have committed!

They have fashioned themselves
gods of gold!

Oh, Lord, please forgive them!

And, if that just is not possible,
please take me off Your list!

Exodus 33:12-16 – a prayer of Moses

Lord, You told me to pilot Your people,
but You haven't told me who will help!

You told me You know me
and favor me in Your sight,
so if I heard You right, please
teach me Your Way to go.

The people You asked me to lead
belong to You, so we need You
to go with us!

Your Presence will let everyone know
we have found favor with You.

Your Presence will distinguish us
from those who follow their own way.

Numbers 6:24-26 – the prayer of Aaron

Lord, we pray You bless and keep us.

We pray Your face shines graciously upon us.

*We pray You look kindly toward us
and give us Your God-peace.*

Shalom.

Numbers 10:35 – a prayer of Moses

Arise, O Lord,
and scatter Your enemies!

Let all who hate You
flee before Your Presence.

Numbers 11:11-15 – a prayer of Moses

Lord, why, oh, why
have You allowed
this trouble to come upon me?

Have I displeased You so much
that You laid on me the burden
of so many people?

Am I a parent to this crowd?
Did I give them birth?

And yet You're asking me
to be their nurse-mate
and carry them like infants
into the earth-place You promised.

How can I look after such a throng,
crying for me to provide?
I cannot take care of them by myself.
This is too much work for one person!

If this is the way it's going to be,
then please do away with me!
I cannot face this trouble alone.

Numbers 12:13 – a prayer of Moses

I'm crying out to You
as loud as Moses:

*Lord God, please
heal my family!*

Numbers 14:17-19 – a prayer of Moses

Lord, I need evidence of Your power!

*You said You're slow to anger
and filled with unfailing love,
forgiving all sorts of sin and rebellion,
yet not excusing the guilty.*

*Indeed, when parents sin, their choices
and actions affect other people–
even a great-great-grandchild!*

*But please pardon us, Lord!
Please keep on parenting us
with Your glorious love.*

Numbers 27:16-17 – a prayer of Moses

Lord God, to everyone
You breathe the breath of life.

Please give us good leaders,
so we will not be
shepherdless sheep.

Deuteronomy 3:24 – a prayer of Moses

Lord God, You have shown me
Your greatness and power.

Where in heaven
or on earth
is there any god
but You who can do
such mighty deeds?

Deuteronomy 9:26-29 – a prayer of Moses

O Lord God, You have redeemed Your people.

Your mighty hand has released us from all that
enslaved us, so please don't do away with us now!

Think about Your faithful servants who came before us
and forget about the stubbornness – the wickedness
so obvious at this moment. Otherwise, people will say
You weren't able to help or give us what You promised.

They'll say You hate us and brought us to this place
to die. But, Lord, we are Your people, Your family –
the ones You rescued with Your enormous power
and open arms.

Deuteronomy 21:8 – a prayer of Moses

Lord, You freed us!
Now please
make peace with us.

Don't let the guilt
of unsolved offenses
reside with Your people.

Give us peace, Lord.
Give us peace.

Deuteronomy 26:10 – a prayer of Moses

Here, Lord!
I'm giving You the first fruits
of the work You have given me.

I'm setting what I have before You
in worship of You –
my Lord and my God.

Judges 5:31 – a prayer of Deborah

May all Your enemies perish, Lord!

May all Your friends shine
like the sun –
rising with strength
and might!

Judges 6:13-17 – a prayer of Gideon

If the Lord is with us,
why
has all this happened?

Where
are the miracles we've heard about
from other people You have rescued?

But now, Lord,
we feel abandoned by You – and yet
You want me to do something to help?

How can I rescue a country?

My family has no influence, and I'm
the least important member anyway.

I hear You say You'll be with me
and give me success in all You ask,

but Lord,
would You please give me a sign
that it's really You I'm talking to?

Judges 13:8 – a prayer of Manoah

Lord,
please
send again
Your
messenger
to teach us
what we're
to do
for this child
You're giving us.

Judges 16:28 – a prayer of Samson

God Almighty, please
keep me in mind!

Give me strength
one more time.

Help me to see
Your work in me.

1 Samuel 2:1-10 – a prayer of Hannah

My heart rejoices in You, Lord!
My very strength praises You.
My mouth speaks confidently
against my opponents, for I gladly rely
on Your deliverance.

No one is holy like You, Lord!
No god exists besides You.
Not even the strongest rock
compares to You, God.

We have nothing to boast about –
no cause to be proud, no room
for a head filled with arrogance.
You, O Lord and God of knowledge,
weigh our actions.

The weapons of the mighty shatter,
but You gird Your children with strength.
Some people hire themselves out to be fed,
but Your children have no cause to hunger.

People with no children might have youth around,
but people with many children might pine for them.

You can kill, Lord, or make alive.
You can bring people down
to the lowest depths or raise them up.
You can give us wealth or poverty.

You might bring us low, but You also
lift us from the dust, the ash heap,
and place us in noble positions, in seats of honor.

Lord, You hold up everything that upholds the earth!

You set the world on high and keep the godly
but silence ill will to darkness.

People cannot prevail on their own,
and those who assert themselves against You
will be shattered by Your booming voice.

You, Lord, will judge every inch of the earth,
but You will strengthen Your leaders
and lift up Your anointed.

1 Samuel 3:10 – a prayer of Samuel

Speak, Lord,
for Your servant
is listening.

1 Samuel 30:8 – a prayer of David

*Shall I keep going
in this direction, Lord?*

Will I succeed?

2 Samuel 7:18-29 – a prayer of David

Lord God, who am I and who is my family
that You have honored me? Maybe
it's a small thing to You, Lord God, but You
have given me a word of hope for the future –
a revelation for all mankind!

What more can I say? You know me,
and You have revealed Your will to me
and given me Your word!

How great You are, Lord God! No one
is like You. No god can stand beside You.

And who are we? You came to us,
ready to rescue and make Your Name known
and perform the most awesome acts to drive
other nations and gods away from Your people.
You took us away from what enslaved us. You
established us forever and have become our God.

Now, Lord God, fulfill Your promise to me
and my family. Do as You have promised, so
we can exalt Your Name forever whenever
anyone says, "The Lord of Hosts is God!"
When You said You will build my family a home,
You gave me courage to pray this prayer.

Lord God, You are God, and Your words
speak only truth. Now, please bless my family
and keep us in You forever – for You, Lord God,
have spoken, and with Your blessings,
we will be blessed.

2 Samuel 22:26-30, 36, 40, 50 – a prayer of David

With the faithful, You prove Yourself faithful, Lord.
With the blameless, You show Yourself blameless,
and those who are pure, see Your purity!

You save the humble,
but humble the proud.

You, my Lord, are my lamp,
illuminating me.

You give me strength,
and with You, I can leap over a wall!

You have shielded me with Your salvation.
Your help has lifted me.

You have clothed me with strength
to battle every trial; You give me victory.

I will give thanks to You everywhere!
I will sing my praise of You.

2 Samuel 24:10 – a prayer of David

*Lord, I have sinned
in what I've done.
Please, O Lord,
remove
this stain on me
for I have acted
foolishly.*

1 Kings 3:6-9 – a prayer of Solomon

You have shown great love
to my family who serve You,
who live in Your presence
with truthful words, integrity,
and a commitment to You.

Now You have shown Your great love
for me by lifting me up to serve.

Lord, my God, I feel as untried
as a child, and yet You've placed me
in a position of leadership
among Your people – the ones You
have chosen – too many to count!

Help my heart to listen, Lord,
so I can know what's fair and right,
so I can discern what's just and good.

1 Kings 8:23-24 – a prayer of Solomon

O Lord, God of Israel,
no god like You exists
anywhere –

not in all of heaven above
or earth below.

You keep Your promises
and show unfailing love
to all who live,
attentively
devoted to You.

1 Kings 8:27-30 – a prayer of Solomon

God, will You really live
with us on earth?

The entire cosmos
cannot hold all of You –
how much less the building
where we hope to meet!

Please listen to my prayer,
O Lord my God.
Hear my cry and pleas.

I pray for You to watch over
our gathering place –
night and day – because You said
Your Name will be with us.

I pray for this sanctuary.

Even if our words are humble,
we earnestly pray You will hear us.

Yes, Lord, hear us and forgive.

1 Kings 8:31-39 – a prayer of Solomon

If
one person allegedly treats another badly, requiring
an Oath of Innocence sworn by Your altar, then hear
from heaven, Lord, and judge between the accuser
and accused. Punish the guilty. Acquit the innocent.
If
Your people sin and suffer defeat from enemies, and
if
they turn to You and acknowledge Your Name and
pray to You in this place, then hear from heaven,
forgive the sin, and return Your people to their land.
If
You shut the skies and lock up the rain because Your
people sinned, but
if
they pray in Your presence and acknowledge Your Name
and turn from wrongdoings because of Your correction, then
hear from heaven and forgive the offense of Your servants.
Teach Your people to follow the path You've shown them.
Send rain on the land You have given as a special possession.
If
the land suffers famine, plague, crop diseases, and attacks
by caterpillars and locusts, or
if
enemies come to the land of Your people, besieging towns –
no matter what the disaster or disease descends – and
if
Your people pray about these troubles, raising their hands
to You in prayer, then hear from heaven where You live
and forgive. Give Your people what their actions deserve
for You alone, Lord, know the human heart.

1 Kings 8:41-43 – a prayer of Solomon

Someday, Lord, people who do not belong
to You will learn of You.

Your Name will draw them from distant lands
for they will hear of Your great Name and strength.

And when they pray in Your presence, hear them
from heaven where You live, and grant what they ask.

Then, all people on earth will eventually
come to know and awe You as Your people do now!

They, too, will see the sanctuary honors Your Name.

1 Kings 8:44-52 – a prayer of Solomon

If
Your people follow Your lead in fighting their enemies, and

if
they pray to You, Lord, by turning toward the place You have chosen and the sanctuary built to honor Your Name, then hear their prayers from heaven and uphold their cause.

If
they sin against You – and who hasn't? – You might get angry over their actions and let conquering enemies take them to another land, but in their exile, they might turn to You, repenting and praying, "We sinned! We have done terrible things and acted badly." Then,

if
they turn to You with all their heart and soul and, even in enemy territory, turn toward You and honor Your Name, then hear their prayers and pleas from Your dwelling place, and uphold their cause. Forgive Your people who have sinned again You. Forgive the offenses committed against You. Make their captors show mercy, for they are Your people, Your special children, whom You redeemed from all that enslaved them.

Lord, open Your eyes to my prayers and the prayers of Your people. Hear and answer us when we cry out to You.

1 Kings 17:20-21 – a prayer of Elijah

O, Lord, my God! Why
have You allowed such tragedy
to people who have been kind to me?

O, Lord, my God,
please restore Your life in them.

1 Kings 18:36-37 – a prayer of Elijah

O, Lord God of my ancestors,
a time of offering draws near.

Now, let everyone know
You are God,
and I am here to serve You
in obedience to Your word.

Answer me, O Lord, answer me,
so people who gather will know
You are Lord.

You are God, and only You
can turn hearts back to You.

2 Kings 6:17 – a prayer of Elijah

*Lord, please open the eyes
of Your servants.*

Help us to see Your help.

*Let us know
You have us covered!*

2 Kings 19:15-19 – a prayer of Hezekiah

Lord of Heavenly Hosts,
God of Israel,
You are enthroned over the angels.
Only You, God of all kingdoms
have made heaven and earth.

Incline Your ear toward me, Lord,
and listen.
Open Your eyes, Lord, and see.

Do You hear the threats sent
to defy You, the living God?

It's true that godless countries
have wiped out many nations,
but their gods aren't real!
They're made of wood and stone
by human hands, and they did not
protect anyone who worshiped them.
Now godless nations have destroyed
their false gods!

Lord, our God, deliver us from evil.
Let all the kingdoms on earth know
You alone are the Lord.

(Compare with Isaiah 37:16-20.)

2 Kings 20:3 – a prayer of Hezekiah

Lord, do You remember me?

Do You recall how I have walked
with You –
                    loyally,
without holding back?

Do You know I want to do
only what pleases You?

(Compare with Isaiah 38:3.)

1 Chronicles 4:10 – a prayer of Jabez

God of Israel, I pray for You
to bless me and increase
my borders.

I ask You to keep Your hand on me
and keep me from painful harm.

1 Chronicles 29:10-19 – a prayer of David

How blessed You are, O Lord God,
forever and ever!

For Yours is the kingdom and the power
and the glory, the victory, and the majesty
over every part of heaven and earth.

You are King of Your people
and head over all.

Riches and honor come from You
as You rule with power and might.

Your hand empowers and strengthens,
and so, You, our God we thank.

We praise Your wondrous Name.

But who am I? Who are my people
to receive Your generosity?
For all things come from You,
and Your hand has given good gifts.

Like our ancestors before us,
we're merely occupants of earth.

Our lifespan is like a passing shadow
without hope of more, but we give
from Your abundance, O Lord,
to make a place for You and Your holy Name.

Everything comes from Your hand!
Everything belongs to You.

You see into our hearts, Lord,

and You know we willingly, gladly,
joyfully offer back to You these gifts.

O Lord God of Abraham, Isaac, Israel,
keep our intentions and motives pure!

Direct our hearts and minds to obey
Your commandments, laws, and rulings
and prepare a place for You to dwell among us.

2 Chronicles 14:11 – a prayer of Asa

Lord God, no one but You
can help both
the mighty and the weak!

Help us, Lord God,
for we depend on You
as we move against evil
in Your Name.

Almighty God,
You are our God.
Let nothing and no one
hinder You.

2 Chronicles 20:6-12 – a prayer of Jehoshaphat

O Lord, God of our ancestors,
You alone are our God in Heaven.
You rule all kingdoms of the earth.
No one can stand against
Your power and might!

You gave a home to the family of Abraham.
Your people settled in this holy land and built
a Temple to honor Your Name.

Whenever hardships came, they promised
to stand in Your presence –
in the place where Your Name is honored,
knowing You hear their cries and will rescue.

But see what armed forces of ill will are doing!
We brought them no harm,
but see how they repay us!
They want to toss us out of the place You've given.

O, God, will You stop them?
We have no power against such strong forces.
We do not know what to do but turn to You.

Ezra 9:5-8 – a prayer of Ezra

*I'm ashamed, Lord God. I'm too
embarrassed to even look at You!*

*My sins and the sins of my people –
Your people –
have piled up enough guilt to reach
to heaven.*

*From the time of our forefathers and mothers,
we have been mired in guilt.*

*Our pastors, priests, and political leaders
have been handed up for execution, and all
our people have been enslaved, robbed,
or disgraced because of our sins.*

*And yet,
for a while anyway, You've kindly left some
survivors with a hold in Your holy place.*

*You made our eyes light up!
You revived us, Lord, even though we're slaves.*

Ezra 9:10-15 – a prayer of Ezra

O, my God! What can we say?
We ignored Your commandments –
the very laws You gave to guide us
through Your servants, the prophets.

They warned us to expect pollution
by perverted people whose disgusting
practices filled the land with wickedness.
They warned us not to intermarry nor
trade peacefully with them.

They said we'd then be strong with all
the goodness this land produces, and
eventually we'd have a long-lasting
inheritance to give Your children and ours.

So much has happened since then
because of our terrible choices and
overwhelming guilt, yet You, our God,
have punished us much less than we
deserve. You have allowed many of us
to survive. If we go back to what we've
been doing, though, and marry people
who do disgusting things You said not
to do, then You might give up on us
and let us be destroyed!

O, my Lord God, You kindly left some
of us as survivors, but look at us!
We have fallen, and none of us
can stand tall in Your presence.

Nehemiah 1:5-11 – a prayer of Nehemiah

Lord, God of heaven,
great and awesome God,
how faithfully
You keep your promise! You
show mercy to those who love You
and obey.
Open Your eyes, and listen
to what I'm praying for Your servants.

Yes, I confess we have sinned against You
as did our families before us.
We have wronged You.
We have not obeyed the commandments
and laws You gave us through Moses.

Remember what You told him? You said,
"If you're unfaithful to Me, I will scatter you,
but if you return to Me and obey – even
if you're far, far away – I will come for you
and bring you to the place I've chosen
to put My Name."

Lord, these are Your people – Your servants,
whom You have saved before, so I'm asking You
to please pay attention to my prayer
and the prayers of all Your servants who want
to worship Your Name. Please give us success,
and show us compassion.

Nehemiah 4:4-6 – a prayer of Nehemiah

Did You hear, God?
We are despised!

We're being demoralized
for trying to rebuild.

What we've done might be
only half as good as before,
but Your people have a mind
to work.

Nehemiah 9:5-6 – a prayer of the people of Israel

The religious leaders called out:

Stand up!
Praise your God,
for the Lord lives on and on
forever!

And the people prayed:

We praise Your glorious Name.
You are higher, Lord, than any
praise or blessing.

You alone are the Lord, Who
made the skies and heavens
and stars.

You made the earth
and seas and everything in them.

You preserve Your creation,
and the angels of heaven
worship You.

Nehemiah 9:9-15 – a prayer of the people of Israel

Lord God, You saw our misery.
You heard our cries.
You demonstrated Your signs,
wonders, and miracles.

What a glorious reputation You have!
You split open the sea, so we
could walk through.
Then You hurled our enemies
into the deep water where
they sank like rocks.

You led us by a pillar of cloud by day
and a pillar of fire by night,
lighting the way You wanted us to go.
From the heavens, You came down
to Mount Sinai and spoke to us,
giving us Your laws and good decrees.

You instructed us to keep the Sabbath
wholly devoted to You.
You encouraged Your people to obey.

When we hungered, You fed us bread
from heaven.
When we grew weary with thirst,
You gave us water from a rock!

You refreshed us and told us to go
take hold of the gifts You promised.

Nehemiah 9:16-21 – a prayer of the people of Israel

How proud our ancestors!
How stubbornly they ignored Your commands.
They refused to obey!
They did not remember the miracles
You had done for them!
They even asked their leader to take them
back into slavery!

But, God, You are forgiving, gracious,
and merciful –
slow to get angry but loaded with love
that does not fail.
You did not abandon Your people –
even when they blasphemed Your Name
and made themselves an idol of gold!

In Your boundless mercy,
You did not desert Your people nor
consign them to death in the wilderness.
The pillar of cloud continued to lead by day,
and the pillar of fire lit the way all night.

Your sent Your good Spirit to instruct,
and You kept providing heavenly bread
and water. For forty years, Your people
lacked nothing! You sustained them
in the wilderness where their clothes did
not tatter. Their feet did not swell!

Nehemiah 9:32-37 – a prayer of the people of Israel

O, great and awesome God –
our mighty God, Who keeps each promise
of unfailing love,
please don't let our present hardships
seem small to You.

Enormous troubles have come upon us
and all Your people!

Whenever You have corrected us,
You have been totally just for we have
greatly sinned, and You only gave us
the chastisement we deserved.

Our leaders, priests, and pastors –
all Your people – have not listened
to Your warnings nor obeyed.

What a huge, lush, lavish land You gave us!
Yet we still acted badly toward You.
So now – surrounded by delicious sources
of food and water, we have become slaves
to ourselves.

Our sins have power over us
and even affect our herds and flocks!
What misery we have brought
upon ourselves!

Nehemiah 13:14 – a prayer of Nehemiah

Remember, my God,
all I have done!

Don't erase
my good work
on behalf of Your House

nor forget
my worship there.

Job 7:17-21 – a prayer of Job

Who are we that You magnify us?

Why are You concerned?

*Why do You examine us every morning
and test us every moment?*

Will You ever stop inspecting me?

*Will You just leave me alone – or
at least give me time to swallow?*

Have I sinned, O Watcher of Men?

What have I done to You?

*Why have You made me Your target
and a burden, even to myself?*

*Why don't You pardon whatever
You think I did wrong and take away
the evil around me? I'm lying down
in dirt, but when You look for me again,
I might be gone!*

Job 9:25-35 – a prayer of Job

*My life sprints by like a runner – so swiftly
it's hard to catch a glimpse of happiness.
Life vanishes like a speedy little boat made of paper
or like an eagle swooping down on its prey.
If I made up my mind to forget my complaints
and put away a sad face to be cheerful,
I would still shudder with pain.*

*O, God, I know You'll never say I'm innocent!
No matter what, I will be found guilty,
so why should I even try?*

*If I scoured myself with soap
and washed my hands with lye,
You might thrust me into a muddy ditch,
so even my clothes would hate my filth!*

*God, You're not a regular person like me,
so how can I argue my case? How can I
take You to trial?*

*Oh, if only a Mediator stood between us –
someone who could bring us together again,
someone who would make You stop
thrashing me, so I would no longer live
in fear of Your chastisement.*

*Then I could talk with You and be unafraid,
but I have no strength to do this alone.*

Job 10:1-12 – a prayer of Job

*I'm so sick and tired of life, I need to complain freely
and rid my soul of bitterness.
God, don't just condemn me!
Tell me the charges You have against me.
What could You possibly gain by keeping me down?
Why would You reject me whom You have made
while letting the wicked get by with their plans?*

*Do You see as I see?
Do You see as people do?*

*Is Your lifetime no longer than ours?
Is Your life so short You must hurry to probe my guilt
and search out my sin when You know I am not guilty!*

*But no one can rescue me from Your hands –
hands that made me but now seem to want to destroy.
Remember? You created me from dust. Will You
turn me back to dust so soon?
You guided my life from first conception
and shaped me in the womb.
You knitted my bones with sinew then clothed me
with soft tissue and skin.
You once gave me life, and showed me
Your loving mercy.
My very being has been preserved by Your care.*

Job 40:3-5 – a prayer of Job

*I'm nobody, Lord, so how
could I possibly think I'd find
answers to my questions about You?*

*I'll put my hand over my mouth.
I've said way too much, Lord!
What else is there to say?*

Job 42:1-6 – a prayer of Job

Lord, I know You can do anything!
No plan of Yours can be thwarted.

You asked why my ignorance hides
me from seeing Your view.
All I can say is, I didn't understand
things too wonderful to know.

You told me to listen,
and You would speak.

You told me to answer Your questions
as I wanted You to answer mine!

I've heard a lot about You, Lord,
but now I've seen You for myself.

And so I take back my words
that questioned You, and I
repent in dust and ashes.

Psalm 3 – a prayer of David

*O Lord, people who wish me harm
are on the rise!
They're saying my soul has no hope
of deliverance from You.*

*But You, O Lord, shield me
with Your glory and lift my head.*

*I cried to You as loud as I could,
and You answered me from Your holiness.
I finally slept and awoke to no harm.*

*Because You sustain me, Lord, I need not fear
the tens of thousands of people
who have set themselves against me.*

*Arise, O Lord. Save me, my God.
You have struck my enemies on the cheek
and kept them from tearing into me.*

*My salvation belongs to You, Lord!
May Your blessing be on all Your people.*

Psalm 4:1-3, 6-8 – a prayer of David

When I call You, O God, please respond!
You said I'm innocent, but I'm troubled.

Have mercy and hear my prayer.
People are trying to ruin my reputation
with groundless accusations!
Must they be allowed to continue in these lies?

I'm sure of this though:
You have set apart the godly as Your own,
so surely You will answer when I call.

Shine Your face toward us, Lord.
You have given me joy greater
than an abundance of bread and wine.

In peace I can lie down to sleep,
for You alone, O Lord, keep me in safety.

Psalm 5 – a prayer of David

Open Your ears to my words, O Lord.
Give thought to what I'm thinking.

Notice my cry for help, my King and my God,
because to You alone do I pray.

Hear me, O Lord, in the morning
when I lay my concerns before You
and wait.

You are not one of those supposed deities
who loves to witness wickedness.
Never do You welcome evil.

You don't want anyone standing around,
bragging or stirring up trouble.
You stop liars from lying,
and You show Your disgust
of cruelness and deceit.

Because of Your great mercy,
I will enter Your dwelling place
and bow reverently to You.

Level Your way in front of me.
O Lord, lead me in Your righteousness
so all who spy on me can see.
Nothing that comes out of their mouths
can be the truth!
From their hearts comes destruction!
Their throats are like an opening
to a tomb, and yet they flatter.
Condemn their actions, Lord.
Let them be brought down
by their own sordid schemes –

brought low by their own crimes
and rebellion against You.

Let all rejoice who look to You
for safety.

Let them sing joyfully forever.

Protect them, and let all who love
Your Name be triumphant.

Like an all-encompassing shield, O Lord,
You surround Your people with favor.

Psalm 6 – a prayer of David

O Lord, don't rebuke me when You're angry
or correct me in Your wrath!
Show me compassion, Lord, for I am weak.

Heal me, Lord, for my very bones are in agony,
and I feel sick at heat!

How long will it be, Lord, until You restore me?
Return, O Lord. Rescue me. Save me with Your
unfailing love.
The dead cannot remember You nor praise You
from the grave.

I am weary from crying all night.
I flood my bed with weeping –
drenching my pillow with tears.
Grief blurs my vision and exhausts my eyes
because of all my enemies.
I just want them to go away!

But, You, Lord have heard my cries.
You have heard my pleas.
You will answer my prayers.

May my enemies be ashamed of themselves.
May terror turn them back in disgrace.

Psalm 7:1-9 – a prayer of David

I need Your protection, O Lord, my God.
Save me! Rescue me from those who persecute.
Otherwise, they will maul me like a lion
and tear me to pieces for I have no one to help.

O Lord, my God, if I have done something wrong
or have been unjust or betrayed a friend
or robbed my enemy, then let my foes capture me.
Let them drag me and my honor into the dirt.

Arise, O Lord! Get angry!
Stand up to the fury of my foes!
Wake up. Bring justice, my God.

Gather the nations to You and rule over them –
judge them, but pronounce me innocent, Lord,
for I want to be righteous, O my Almighty God!

Stop the cruel behavior of the wicked,
and defend those who try to do right by You.
You know who, for You look all the way
into the mind and heart, O righteous God.

Psalm 8 – a prayer of David

*O Lord, our Lord, how excellent is
Your Name in all the earth!*

*Your glory rises higher than the heavens,
yet You have given strength to the songs
of babies and to children who sing
with power, silencing Your enemies!*

*When I consider the heavens –
the finger-work You have made
of stars and moon – I wonder why
people are so important to You.
What are human beings that You
are so mindful of us?*

*For we're lower than angels, yet
You crowned us with glory and honor!
You put us in charge of all You've made.
You have given us dominion to rule
and take kindly care of the sheep,
cattle, and beasts of the field,
the birds of the air, the fish of the sea,
and whatever comes along!*

*O Lord, our Lord, how excellent
is Your Name in all the earth!*

Psalm 9:1-10 – a prayer of David

Here I am, Lord,
praising You with all my heart,
telling about the marvelous things You do.

Because of You, joy fills me,
and I sing praises to Your Name,
O Most High!

My enemies pull away.
They stagger and gasp as You appear,
as You rule in my favor.
From Your throne, You judge with fairness.
The nations feel Your rebuke.
You destroy the wicked and erase their names.
You leave Your enemies in endless ruins –
uprooted and forgotten.

But You, Lord, reign forever.
From Your throne, You send forth justice,
ruling the nations with fairness.

What a shelter You are in times of trouble –
a refuge for the oppressed!

Anyone who truly knows You will trust You,
for You, O Lord, do not abandon those who seek You.

Psalm 10:1, 12, 14-18 – a prayer of David

Why are You so far away, Lord?
Why are You hiding in this troubling time?

Rise up! Lift up Your hand, Lord God!
Remember the afflicted.

You, too, have seen trouble and grief.
You detect and observe it
before taking the matter into Your hands.

Powerless people entrust themselves to You.
You help the fatherless.
You break the hold of evil,
calling wicked behavior into account
until nothing of it remains.

You, Lord, are King forever and ever,
but others will perish from the land.

You hear the desires of the humble, Lord.
You listen carefully
and strengthen their hearts.
You provide justice for the most vulnerable,
so no one can terrify them again.

Psalm 12:1-3, 6-7 – a prayer of David

Help, Lord!

Is there anyone still faithful to You?
Has all sense of loyalty disappeared?

People lie to each other
and flatter and deceive.
Stop them, Lord!

Whatever You say is purer than silver
refined seven times by fire.

Guard us, Lord.
Protect us in these terrible times.

Psalm 13 – a prayer of David

Are You going to forget me forever, Lord?

How long will You look away?

*How long must my soul wrestle with anguish,
my heart with sorrow? Every day?*

How long will those against me have the upper hand?

*Turn to me! Answer me, O Lord my God!
Rekindle my hope, my spark, or I will die!*

*Don't let anyone gloat over me, saying, "We won!"
Don't let them celebrate my downfall.*

I trust Your unfailing love.

I rejoice, remembering You have rescued me.

I will sing to You, Lord, for You are good to me.

Psalm 16:1, 5-11 – a prayer of David

Keep me out of harm's way, O God,
for I've come to You for safe haven.

You alone are my legacy,
my cup of blessing.
You guard all that is mine.

What a pleasant place You have given me!
What a wonderful inheritance!

God bless You, Lord, for guiding me.
Even at night, You instruct my heart.

I know You are always with me.
With You right here, I will not be shaken!

No wonder my glad heart rejoices,
for I rest in safety, knowing
You will not abandon my soul to death,
nor let Your holy one decay in a grave.

You will show me The Way of Life in You,
granting me joy in Your presence
and the pleasure of living with You
forever.

Psalm 17:1-9, 13-15 – a prayer of David

Hear my plea for justice, O Lord!
Listen to my cry for Your help.

Pay attention to my prayers
for I speak to You honestly.

Pronounce my innocence
for You see who does right.

You have tested my darkest thoughts,
examined my heart, scrutinized me,
and found nothing wrong,
so I don't want to sin now in what I say,
but I've followed Your commandments,
which kept me from going in erroneous ways.

I've kept my steps on Your path
and have not wavered from following You,
so I'm praying to You because I know
You will answer me, O God. You will
bend down to hear me as I pray.

You show me Your unfailing love
in such wonderful ways!

With Your mighty power, You rescue
those who seek refuge in You.

Guard me as You would shield Your own eyes!

Hide me in the shadow of Your wings.

Protect me from wicked attacks,
by those who surround me with opposition.
Rise up, O Lord!

Stand up and bring these opponents to their knees!

Rescue me with Your sword –
with the power of Your hand, Lord,
and destroy their worldly ways,

but feed the needs of those who treasure You.
May their children have plenty
with Your legacy for their descendants.

Those who aim toward right living will see you.
When I awake, I will see You up close and be glad.

Psalm 18:1-2 – a prayer of David

I love You, Lord!

You are my strength.
You are my rock,
my fortress,
my refuge,
my shield,
my deliverer,
my salvation!

Psalm 19:14 – a prayer of David

*Let the words of my mouth
and the meditations of my heart
be acceptable in Your sight,*

*O Lord, my strength
and my Redeemer.*

Psalm 21:1, 2, 13 – a prayer of David

Our leaders find joy
in Your strength, O Lord.

You give what's wanted,
what's needed.

Supreme power is Yours alone,
Sovereign Lord!

To You, we sing and lift
our songs of praise.

Psalm 22:1-19 – a prayer of David

My God, my God, why have You deserted me?
Why are You so far away when I cry for help?

Every day I call to You, God, but You do not answer.
Every night I lift my voice but find no relief.

And yet, I know You are holy!
You are enthroned on the praises of Your people.

When our ancestors trusted You, You rescued them.
When they cried out to You, You saved.
When they trusted in You, they were not sorry.

But I feel like a worm, not a person!
I'm scorned and despised by too many to count!

Almost everyone who see me mocks me.
They sneer at me and shake their heads, saying,
'Is this the one who relied on the Lord? Let the
Lord save! If the Lord loves him, let the Lord rescue.'

Yes! For You brought me safely from my mother's womb
and led me to trust You – even as a nursing infant.

At my birth, I was given into Your arms,
and You have been my God from that moment,
so don't stay away from me now!

Trouble is near, and no one can help me but You.

My enemies surround me like a herd of animals –
fierce animals fencing me in.

Like lions, they open their jaws against me,
roaring and ready to tear me like prey.

My life pours out like water,
and all my bones slip out of joint

My heart feels like wax, melting within me,
and my strength dries up like sun-baked clay.

My tongue sticks to the roof of my mouth
while You lay me in the dust as though I'm dead.

My enemies surround me like a pack of wild dogs —
like a gang closing in on me.

They pierce my hands and my feet!
I can count all my bones.

People stare and gloat. They divide
my garments among themselves and toss dice
for my clothing.

O Lord, do not stay away!
You alone are my strength. Help me! Come quickly!

Psalm 22:20-31 – a prayer of David

Lord, save me from the sword!

Snatch my precious life
from these dogs, the mouths
of lions, the goring horns of wild oxen.

Then I will proclaim Your Name to everyone!
I will praise You in a gathering of Your people.

Praise the Lord! All who fear God,
show honor. Show reverence.
For You have not ignored us nor belittled
our needs or our suffering.

You have not turned away, God, but have
listened to each cry for help.

Lord, I will praise You in a gathering of Your people.
I will fulfill my vows among those who worship You.

Let the poor eat and be satisfied!

Let all who seek the Lord give praise
for our hearts have cause to rejoice forever.

The whole earth will acknowledge You, Lord,
and return to You. All families –
all nations will bow down to You
for to You belongs the power – the royal power
to rule every nation on earth.

Let the rich eat and worship!

Let all who are mortal – whose lives will end
in dust – submit their lives to the Lord.

May our children also serve You, Lord.

*May future generations always hear
about Your wonders.*

*May Your righteous acts – all You have done –
be told, Lord, to those not yet born.*

Psalm 23 – a prayer of David

Lord, You are my shepherd.
There's nothing I lack.

You make me lie down in lush pastures.
You lead me beside still waters.
You restore my soul.
For the sake of Your Name,
You escort me along Your paths
of righteousness.

Yes, even if I walk through a valley,
shadowed by death, I need not fear evil
for You are with me!
Your shepherd's rod and staff
bring me security and comfort.

You prepare a banquet before me
in the presence of my enemies!
You anoint my head with oil.
You fill my cup to overflowing!

Surely Your goodness and mercy
shall be with me every day of my life,
and I will dwell with You forever.

Psalm 25:1-7, 11, 16-22 – a prayer of David

I lift my soul to You, O Lord.
I trust You!

Do not let me be put to shame.
Don't let anyone put me down.

Let no one ever be ashamed
of waiting for You.

Make known to me Your ways, O Lord.
Teach me Your paths.

Lead me into Your truth with Your instruction
because You are my God, my savior,
for Whom I'll wait all day!

I remember Your compassion
and merciful deeds infinitely shown,
but I don't want You to remember
my bad judgment as a youth
nor my rebellion against You.

Bring me to mind instead, Lord,
along the lines of Your mercy,
Your goodness!

Remove my great guilt, O Lord,
for the sake of Your good Name!

Turn to me with empathy
for I feel lonely and oppressed.

Relieve the troubles of my heart,
and lift me from distress.

See my misery and suffering?
Forgive my sins.

See the ill will increasing around me?
How viciousness surrounds me with hate!

Protect my life!
Rescue me!

Let me never be ashamed
of taking refuge in You.

Let Your integrity and truth
protect me as I wait for You.

O God! Rescue Your people
from our troubles!

Psalm 26:1-3 – a prayer of David

Judge me, O Lord!

I aim to walk
upright and honest,
and I trust You
to keep me from sliding.

Prove me.
Try me.
Test me.
Look closely
into my heart and mind.

Before my eyes –
Your steadfast love…!

Before my steps –
Your truth…!

Psalm 27:8-12 – a prayer of David

My heart tells me to come and seek
Your face, O Lord, and Your face
do I seek.

Please, don't hide!
Don't turn away!
Don't abandon me –
ever!

Even if my parents leave,
You will not forsake me.
You will take me up.

Teach me Your way, O Lord.
Level the path before me.
Do not give me up!

Psalm 30:1-3 – a prayer of David

Out of my troubles,
You lifted me, Lord.

I prayed to You,
my Lord, my God,
and You healed me!

You brought my soul up
from Sheol.

You brought me up,
so I wouldn't dwell
in the pits!

You saved
my life.

Psalm 31:1-5 – a prayer of David

I'm putting my trust in You, Lord.
Let me never be ashamed
of trusting You!

I count on Your righteousness
to deliver me.
Please keep inclined to listen.

Carry me quickly into the place
of Your defense.
For You are my rock.

You're like a fortress –
a fortified castle –
Who keeps me housed
in safety.

Guide me, Lord,
for Your Name's sake.
You are the way
out of trouble!

Into Your hands
I commit my spirit.

Psalm 33:22 – a prayer of David

Rest Your mercy
on us, Lord,
as we wait
in hope for
You.

Psalm 35:1-5, 9-10, 17-19, 22-28 – a prayer of David

Contend, O Lord, with those who contend with me.
Fight against those who fight against me.
Hold up Your buckler and shield, and rise to protect me!
Draw Your spear and weapons against those who pursue me.

Remind my very soul that You are my salvation.

Let anyone who seeks my life be ashamed of themselves!
Let anyone with evil aims be stopped and humiliated!
Let their ill intents be blown away like chaff –
like Your angels shooing away trouble!

Let my soul rejoice in You, Lord.
Let my deepest self celebrate Your salvation.

My very bones say, "Lord, who is like You?
Who else can deliver the afflicted from a strong opponent?
Who else can keep the poor from being further robbed?"

How long will You watch all of this, Lord?
Rescue my soul, my life from being torn by beasts!

I promise to thank You in a great assembly
and praise You among a mighty throng of people!
Just don't let anyone rejoice wrongfully over me.
Don't let them hate me or wink malice without cause.

You've seen it all, Lord. Oh, please do not keep silent!
Oh, please do not be far from me, Lord.
Stir Yourself awake for me and my reasoning,
for You are my Lord and my God.

Judge me, O Lord, my God, according to Your truths,
but do not let anyone rejoice over my misfortune.
Do not let beastly people try to swallow me up!

Let anyone who celebrates my distress be ashamed and humiliated. Clothe with shame and dishonor anyone who acts as though they're better than me, but let everyone who want to see things get better shout for joy and celebrate my acquittal.

Let them say – over and over – "May You, Lord, be magnified and delighted in the success of Your servants."

Then I will tell everyone of Your righteousness.
I will praise You again and again.

Psalm 36:5-11 – a prayer of David

O Lord, Your loving kindness extends to the heavens.
Your faithfulness reaches the skies.
Your righteousness rises like mountains.
Your judgments go into great depth.

O Lord, You preserve people and animals.

How precious is Your loving kindness, O God!
Even young children take refuge
in the shadow of Your wings.

You fill us with abundance from Your house.
You give us a drink from the river of Your delights.

For with You, O Lord, is the fountain of life,
and in Your light we see light.

Please keep on showing Your loving kindness
to those who yearn to know You – the upright
in heart who want to know Your righteous ways.

Don't let me swagger along in pride!
Let nothing wicked drive me from You.

Psalm 38 – a prayer of David

O Lord, don't rebuke me when You're angry
nor discipline me in rage!

Your arrows struck deep. Your blows pound me!
Because I've displeased You, my whole body feels sick.

Sin has broken my health.

My guilt overwhelms me—
a burden too weighty to bear.

My wounds fester and stink
because of my foolishness.

Pain racks me until I'm bent over!
All day I walk around in grief.

A burning fever rages within
and breaks.

I'm exhausted and completely crushed.
My heart groans with anguish,
but what I long for, Lord,
is for You to hear my cries, my sigh.

How wildly my heart beats!
my strength fails, and I can barely see.

My friends and loved ones stay away,
fearing I might infect them!
My own family stands at a distance
while enemies lay traps to do away with me.

Those who wish me harm plan to ruin me.
They plan treachery, but I don't listen to their threats.

I am silent before them as one who cannot speak.
I choose to hear nothing and make no reply,
for I am waiting for You, Lord.

O Lord, my God, answer on my behalf! Don't let
my enemies gloat over me or rejoice at my downfall."

I'm about to collapse with this chronic pain, and yet I
confess my sins for I am deeply sorry for what I've done.

Many aggressive foes hate me for no reason. They repay
good with evil and challenge me for pursuing what is right.

Do not abandon me, Lord!
Do not stand at a distance, my God.
Come quickly to help me, O Lord, my Savior.

Psalm 39:4-13 – a prayer of David

Teach me, O Lord, about the end of my life.
Teach me how many days I have left,
so I may realize how temporary my life is.
You have measured my length of days in inches!
My life span isn't very big in Your sight.
Everyone alive is like a whisper of wind.
Every person who walks around is only a shadow,
busy for no real reason, accumulating possessions
without knowing who will get them.

Lord, what else should I be waiting for?
My hope is in you!
Rescue me from my own rebellion.
Do not disgrace me in front of godless people.
I remained silent. I did not open my mouth
because You have prepared this!

Take away the sickness You laid upon me.
My life is over if You strike me with Your hand!
Your stern warnings discipline people for misdeeds,
and, like a moth, You devour what they treasure.
Everyone alive is like a whisper of wind.

Listen to my prayer, O Lord.
Open Your ear to my cries for help.
Do not hold Your peace at my tears,
for I am Your guest, passing through –
a stranger like my ancestors.
Turn Your gaze from me, so I may smile again
before I disappear and am no more.

Psalm 40:5,6-8 – a prayer of David

How many are Your miracles,
O Lord, my God,
and Your wonderful works!

How many thoughts do You have
of us – too many to count?

You don't want us to bring
sacrificial offerings for our sins.

You want us to come to You
as others have, saying, "Here
I am, Lord! I delight to do Your will.
I keep Your words in my heart."

Psalm 41:4 – a prayer of David

Lord, be merciful to me,
a sinner.

Forgive me.
Heal my soul.

Be gracious to me, Lord.
Lift me up.

Psalm 43 – a prayer of the family of Korah

Tell them I'm innocent, O God!
Defend me against ungodly people.
Rescue me from these liars.

You, my God, are my only safe haven.
Why must You toss me aside?
Why must I wander around in grief,
oppressed by my enemies?

Send out Your light, Your truth,
and let them guide me.

Lead me to Your holy mountain,
the place where You reside,
and I will go to Your altar,
my God – the source of my joy.
I will praise You with my harp.

O God! Why am I so discouraged?
Why does my heart get so sad?

I choose to put my hope in You!
I choose to praise You again—
my Savior and my God!

Psalm 44:1-8 – a prayer of the family of Korah

O God,
we have heard with our own ears what
our ancestors told us about the miracles
You performed in their day – days long ago.

By your power, You uprooted nations
from the land and planted our ancestors.
You shattered many but set our families free.
They did not take possession of the land
nor gain victory with their own strength
but with Your right hand, Your arm.

The light of Your presence did this
for the pleasure You take in Your people.

You alone are my king, O God.
You alone won victories for our ancestors.

With You we can prevail over our enemies.
With Your Name we can crush all who attack.

I don't rely on my bow nor my sword to save.
But You saved us from our enemies
and put to shame those who hate us.

All day long we praise You, God.
We give thanks to You forever.

Psalm 51:1-18 – a prayer of the family of Korah

Be gracious to me, God. In accordance
with Your faithful love and abundant
compassion, blot out my rebellion.

Cleanse me from sin and guilt,
for I am very aware of my rebellion,
and my sin is always before me.

Against You – You alone – have I sinned
and done wrong in Your sight.
So You are right to declare a verdict.

You are blameless when You judge.
From birth, I had a tendency toward guilt,
even when my mother conceived me.
But You want my inner self to have integrity,
and Your wisdom permeates deep within me.

Purify me with hyssop, and I will be clean.
Wash me, and I will be whiter than snow.

Let me live in joy and gladness.
Let the bones You have crushed rejoice.

Turn Your face from my sins and blot out
my guilt, God. Create a clean heart in me
and renew a steadfast spirit within me.

Do not banish me from Your presence,
nor hide Your Holy Spirit from me.

Restore to me the joy of Your salvation,
and give me a spirit willing to do Your will.
Then I will teach Your ways to rebellious
people, and sinners will return to You.

Save me from the blame of bloodshed,
O God of my salvation, and my tongue
will sing of Your righteousness. Open my lips,
Lord, and my mouth will declare Your praise.

If You wanted a sacrifice, I would give it,
but burnt offering do not please You.

The pleasing sacrifice is a receptive spirit,
for You will not despise a humbled heart.

In Your good time, You will cause
Your people to prosper and rebuild
this place You have given to us.

Psalm 54 – a prayer of the family of Korah

Come with great power, O God, and rescue me!

Defend me with Your strength.
Listen to my prayer, O God.
Pay attention to my plea.

For strangers attack me,
and violent people – people who care nothing
for You – try to destroy me.

But You are my helper.
You keep me alive, Lord!

Please turn the evil plans
of my enemies against them.

Do as You promised and put an end to this!

I vow to sacrifice a voluntary offering to You.
I vow to praise Your good Name, O Lord,
for You have rescued me from tight spots
and helped me to triumph over troublers.

Psalm 55:1-16 – a prayer of the family of Korah

Listen to my prayer, O God.
Do not ignore my cry for help!

Please listen and answer me,
for I am overwhelmed by difficulties.

My enemies holler at me,
making loud and hateful threats.
They bring trouble on me
and angrily pursue me.

My heart pounds in my chest.
The terror of death assaults me.
Fear and trembling overcome me,
and I can't seem to stop shaking.

Oh, for wings like a dove,
so I could fly away and rest!
I would fly far away
to the silence of the wilderness.

How quickly, how far I would flee
from this wild storm of hatred!

Confuse and frustrate their plans, Lord,
for I see violence and conflict in the city.
The walls are patrolled day and night
against invaders, but the real danger
is the wickedness within.

Everything is falling apart!
Threats and corruption spill
unbridled in the streets.
And yet, it's not an enemy who taunts me.
I could bear that.

It is not my foes who so arrogantly insult me—
I could hide from them.

No, it is someone like me –
my companion and close friend!

What wonderful fellowship we once enjoyed
as we walked together to the house of the Lord.

Let death hover over my enemies!
Let the grave swallow them whole,
for evil makes its home in them.

But I'm calling on You, God, and You will
rescue me.

Psalm 56:1-4, 8-13 – a prayer of the family of Korah

People are harassing me!
O God, have pity on me.
People who try to start a brawl
keep me down.
People who are against me
spy on me, pester me,
and get ready to fight,
but even though I'm scared,
I trust You, Lord.
I praise Your word.
I trust in You.

What can mere flesh and blood do to me?
For You, Lord, know my comings and goings.
You have kept my tears in a bottle,
in Your record book.

My enemies will retreat when I call You,
for I know: You are on my side.
I praise Your word, Lord God.
I praise Your word.
I trust You, and I am not afraid.
What can mere flesh and blood do to me?

I bind myself to You with vows, O God,
and I will keep my vows by offering You
songs of thanksgiving,
for You have rescued me from death.
You have kept me from stumbling,
so I can walk in Your presence,
in the Light of Life.

Psalm 57:1-3, 8-11 – a prayer of the family of Korah

Be gracious to me, God. Be gracious,
for I hide myself in You.
Until danger passes by, I seek refuge
in the shadow of Your wings.

I call to You, God Most High,
and You fulfill Your purpose for me.
You reach down from heaven
and save me, but challenge those
who try to walk all over me!

Wake up, my soul!
Wake up spheres of music!
I will awaken the dawn,
for I am praising You, Lord,
among all peoples.

I will sing Your praise to all the nations,
for Your steadfast love is as high as
the heavens, and Your faithfulness
reaches the clouds.

Be exalted above the heavens, Lord God.
Let Your glory spread over all the earth.

Psalm 59:1-2, 16-17 – a prayer of the family of Korah

O my God, please rescue me from enemies.
Protect me from my attackers.

Rescue me from makers of trouble.
Save me from anyone out for blood!

Of Your strength, I will sing!

With joy, I will sing
of Your mercies each morning.

You have been my stronghold –
my safe place in times of trouble.

In strength, I will make music to praise You,
for You are my fortress, my merciful God.

Psalm 60:1-5 – a prayer of the family of Korah

O God, have You rejected us?

You have been angry with us
and broken down our defenses.
Restore us now!

You made the land quake
and split open.
Now heal these rifts
before the world falls apart!

You made Your people
quake from hardships
and stagger from the cup
You gave us to drink.

And yet, You have raised a banner
over those who fear You,
so we can rally together
when we're under attack.

Save us with Your hand of power!
Answer us, so those dear to You
may be delivered into safety.

Psalm 61 – a prayer of the family of Korah

O God, are You listening?
Hear my prayer, my cry.
From every part of the earth,
I call to You for help
when I feel overwhelmed.

Lead me to Your tower,
Your rock of safety, for You
are my refuge, my fortress
where nothing harmful
can touch me.

Let me stay here! Let me live
forever in Your holy place, safe
beneath Your sheltering wings.

O God, You heard what I promised,
and You have given me
an inheritance set aside for those
who stand in awe of Your Name.

Give a long life to our leaders –
years spanning generations –
as they reign under Your protection
and as Your unfailing love and loyalty
reign over them.

How I will sing Your praises!
Each day, I will do all I promised You.

Psalm 63:1-4 – a prayer of David

God, You are my God.
I seek You.

My soul withers without You;
my body feels weary and faint.

I've glimpsed You
in the sanctuary.
I have seen Your power and glory.

Your loving kindness is better than life.
My lips shall praise You.

I will bless You as long as I live.
I will lift up my hands in Your Name.

Psalm 64:1-2 – a prayer of David

Hear my voice, O God,
even when I complain!

Protect my life from fear
and dread of terror.

Hide me from hateful plots
and hate-filled people,
from trouble-making mobs.

Psalm 65:1-3 – a prayer of David

Lord God in Zion,
we praise You
and offer You our vows.

O You, Who answers prayers,
to You all flesh will come!

When my guilt becomes
too weighty to bear,
You promise to forgive.

How happy! How blessed
are Your people!

We come into Your court,
satisfied by the goodness
of Your home – the place
where You dwell.

Psalm 69:1-6 – a prayer of David

Save me, O God,
for I am drowning!
Floodwaters rise to my neck.
I sink deeper and deeper into mire.
I can't find a foothold!
I'm in too deep,
and everything overwhelms me.

I'm so tired of crying for help.
My throat is parched and
my eyes swollen from weeping,
waiting for You to help me.

Those who hate me without case
outnumber the hairs on my head!
Many try to destroy me with lies.
They demand I give back what
I never even took!

God, I know You know how foolish
I've been, for my sins cannot
be hidden from You, but, oh
Sovereign Lord of Heaven's Armies,
please do not let anyone who
trusts in You ever be ashamed
because of me. Do not let me
be the cause of their humiliation,
O God of Your people and mine.

Psalm 69:13-21, 29-30 – a prayer of David

*I keep on praying to You, Lord,
hoping You will show me favor.*

*In Your consistent love, O God,
answer my prayer with the truth
of Your salvation.*

*Rescue me from this mire!
Don't let me sink any lower!
Save me from those who wish me ill
and pull me from deep waters.*

*Don't let anything overwhelm me
or bottomless waters swallow me
or death traps devour me!*

*Answer my prayers, O Lord,
for Your wonderful love does not fail.*

Let Your abundant mercy care for me.

*Don't hide from me! Hurry
and answer me, for I am in trouble.*

*Come and redeem me. Free me
from whoever is against me.*

*You know I've been insulted,
humiliated, and disgraced,
for You see what's been brought
against me. Such insults break
my heart, and I am in despair.*

*If only One would show pity!
If only One would turn and comfort me.*

But they give me gall and, for my thirst,
sour wine to drink.

O God, I am suffering and in pain!
Rescue me by Your saving power.

Then I will praise Your Name with songs.
I will honor You by giving my thanks.

Psalm 70 – a prayer of David

Deliver me, God!
Lord, hurry to help me!

Let anyone who seeks my life
be disgraced and confounded.

Let those who wish me harm
be driven away in embarrassment.

Let everyone who seeks You
rejoice and be happy in You.

Let those who love
Your deliverance
keep saying, "God is great!"

But, God, I am in distress
and in need!

You are my help.
You are my deliverer.
Oh please, Lord, do not delay.

Psalm 71:1-12 – a prayer of the family of Korah

I put my trust in You, O Lord.
Help me never to be confused about that.
Rescue me. Free me for You do what's right.
Stay inclined to listen to me and deliver me.
Be to me a Rock where I can safely hide.
Give Your command to rescue me,
for You are my high ridge and fortress.
Rescue me, my God, from the power of evil,
from the clutches of cruel oppressors.

O Lord, my only hope is in You.
From childhood I have trusted You, Lord.
Yes, from the moment of my birth
and even in my mother's womb, You
have tended me.

No wonder I'm always praising You.
No wonder my life provides an example to many,
because You have been my strength and protection.
No wonder I daily declare Your praise and glory!

Now that I'm older, please don't set me aside.
Please don't leave me when my strength fails,
for people whisper against me and plot
to do me in. They say, "God has gone from him!
Let's go get him, for who will help him now?"

O God, please don't stay away.
Please hurry to help me, my God.

Psalm 71:14-23 – a prayer of the family of Korah

*Lord, I'll keep on hoping for Your help
and praising You.*

*I want to tell everyone I know
about Your righteousness
and Your power to save,
although I can't begin to say
nor even understand
how many such acts there are!*

*O, Sovereign Lord, I go in Your strength,
proclaiming Your honesty and virtue –
not mine.*

*You have taught me from early childhood,
and I still tell everyone I know
about the wonders You have done.*

*Now that I'm aging and getting gray,
do not leave me, O God!*

*Let me live to tell the next generation
about You and Your miracles, Your might.*

*O God, Your righteousness reaches
to unknowable heights!*

*What wonders You have done!
No one can compare with You, O God.*

*Yes, You've allowed me to suffer hard times,
but You restore me and lift me up
from the lowest points in my life.
You repair my reputation and will again
comfort me.*

Then my heartstrings will resonate praise,
my God, and proclaim Your faithfulness
to Your vows.

With stringed instruments, I will sing Your praise,
O Holy One of my people.

I will shout with joy and sing Your praises,
for You have set me free.

Psalm 74:1-2, 10-11, 18-23 – a prayer of Asaph

O God, why does it feel like You've rejected us –
forever?
Why does Your displeasure smolder
against those in Your care?

Remember Your people who gather in Your Name?
Long ago, You made us Your own!
You purchased us from slavery
and brought us to our home in You.

How long, O God, will our opponents insult us?
How long will they despise You?
Did You shove Your hands in Your pockets?
Show Your hand of power!

Remember the insults against You, O Lord?
Remember how a godless nation despised Your Name?
Oh, don't hand over the souls of Your doves
to wild animals! Don't forget Your oppressed people.

Think about Your promises
as violence darkens every corner of the land.
Do not let Your people come back
oppressed and disgraced!
We're weak and needy, Lord,
but we praise Your Name.

Rise up, O God!
Fight for Your own cause!
Don't ignore the godless people who insult You,
continually, and shout against You.
Don't ignore the uproar they make in their attacks.

Psalm 75:1 – a prayer of Asaph

We give thanks
to You, O Lord.

We give thanks.
For Your Name
is near.

Your Name
holds wondrous
deeds.

Psalm 79:1-2, 5-13 – a prayer of Asaph

O God, we've been invaded,
desecrated,
ruined!

The corpses of Your servants
have fed the birds of the sky!
The flesh of Your godly ones
has been given to beasts!

How long will this go on, Lord?
Will Your anger and jealousy
burn like an eternal fire?

Pour wrath on those
who do not acknowledge You,
on kingdoms that don't call on Your Name!

Your people and our homeland
are being devastated and devoured!

Please, don't hold old sins against us!
Hasten Your compassion, for we are weak.

God of our salvation, help us for goodness sake!

Deliver us! Let Your Name atone for our sins.
Why should anyone ask, "Where is your God?"

Let us see Your vengeance
for the blood of Your servants,
and let it be known among the nations.

Let the groans of Your enslaved people
reach You.
Let Your great power preserve their lives.

*But, Lord, pay back seven times over
those who rebuke You!*

*Then we, Your people –
the sheep of Your pasture –
will thank You forever
and praise You
from generation to generation.*

Psalm 80 – a prayer of Asaph

Hear me, O Shepherd of Your people, Who leads us like a flock. From Your throne among cherubim, rally Your power, show Your strength, and come to save us. Restore us to Your favor, God, and we will be saved. O Lord God, Commander of Heavenly Armies, how long will You be angry, even with our prayers? You have fed us tears as bread – floods of tears to drink! You made us a source of conflict with our neighbors. Our enemies taunt us.

Restore us to Your favor, God, Commander of Heavenly Armies, and we will be saved.

You uprooted us like a vine from all that enslaved us. You drove out nations to clear a place to plant us. We took root and filled the land. This shade covered mountains; the branches shadowed mighty cedars, sending sprouts toward the Sea, shoots toward the River. Why have You broken down walls, so all who pass by can pick our fruit? Wild pigs from the forest tear up our vines, and creatures of the fields feed on them.

Come back, God, Commander of Heavenly Armies! Look down from heaven and see! Take care of this vine and the root Your right hand planted, the shoot You made strong for Yourself. Cut and burned, what will not wither at Your rebuking look?

Place Your hand on the Son of Man – the One You have chosen, the One You made strong for Yourself. Then we won't turn away from You. Revive us, and we will call on Your Name.

Restore us to Your favor, God, Commander of Heavenly Armies, and we will be saved.

Psalm 83:1-3, 13-18 – a prayer of Asaph

O God, don't be silent!
Don't turn a deaf ear to me.
Don't keep quiet, O God.

Look! Your adversaries roar!
Those who hate You
hold high their heads.
They make secret plans
against Your people.
They plot against those
You treasure.

O my God, make them like
whirling dust, like chaff
in the wind.

Pursue them, terrify them
with storms and wind –
the way fire frightens a forest,
and flames set a mountain on fire.

Let shame cover their faces, O Lord.
Let them die disgraced or be terrified
forever until they look to You for help
and acknowledge Your Name – the Lord.
You alone are the Most High God of all
the earth.

Psalm 84:1-4,10-12 – a prayer of the family of Korah

How lovely is Your dwelling place,
O Lord of Hosts!

My soul longs for You.
When I'm not in Your presence,
I feel like I'll just faint!

Every part of my being
wants to be with You!
I'm crying out for You, my Living God!

Even a sparrow finds a home
and the swallow a nest
where she can raise her young.

How happy we are when we dwell
with You and sing Your praise!

One day in Your court is better
than a thousand days anywhere else,
even if I can only be an usher, a
sentry, or doorkeeper.

Lord God, You bring more light
than the sun, more protection
than a shield.

You hold back nothing good
from those who love You.
How blessed are people
who put their whole trust in You!

Psalm 85:1-8 – a prayer of the family of Korah

What blessings You pour on Your land, O Lord!

You restored the fortunes of Your people
and forgave their guilt. Yes, You covered all
their sins. You withdrew wrath and fierce fury.

Now restore us again, O God of our salvation.
Put aside Your anger toward us.

Will You be mad at us forever?
Will Your anger affect future generations?

Or will You revive us, so Your people
can again rejoice in You?

Show us Your ongoing love, O Lord.
Grant us Your salvation.

Help us to listen
carefully to what You say!
For You, Lord speak peace to faithful people.

Psalm 86:1-10 – a prayer of David

Cup Your ear in my direction, O Lord,
and answer me,
for I am in trouble, and I need You.

Preserve my soul, for I am faithful to You.
O my God, save Your servant who trusts in You.

Be gracious to me, O Lord, for I call to You
all day long.

Gladden my soul, for to You, O Lord,
I lift up my life.

You, Lord, are good and eager to forgive.
Your love and kindness are abundant
to all who call on You.

Give ear, O Lord, to my prayer.
Give heed to my voice, my pleas.

When I'm troubled, I shall call on You,
for You will answer me.

No one else is like You, O Lord,
nor can any do works like Yours.
The nations You created shall come
and worship You, O Lord, and give glory
to Your Name, for You are great.
You do amazing things, for You alone
are God.

Psalm 86:11-17 – a prayer of David

O Lord, if You'll teach me Your way,
I'll walk in Your truth.
Help my heart to be undivided
and totally in awe of Your Name.

With all my heart, I thank You,
O Lord, my God, and I will glorify
Your Name forever, for Your love
and kindness toward me cannot be
measured. You have lifted my soul
from the deepest darkness.

O God, arrogant people have risen up
against me, and, without You to guide,
a violent mob seeks my life.

But You, O Lord, are a God of mercy
and grace, slow to anger, and abundant
in love, kindness, and truth.

Turn to me. Have mercy on me.
Oh, grant the strength I need.
Save me –
the child of Your servant.

Show signs of Your goodness,
so those against me will see and be
ashamed, knowing You, O Lord,
have been my help and comfort.

Psalm 88:1-3, 9-13 – a prayer of the family of Korah

O, my Savior, my Lord, my God,
to You I cry every day and night!

Let my prayer come into Your presence.

Let Your ear hear my cries, for my soul
fills with trouble, and my life gets closer
to death.

Suffering weakens my eyes as I call
to You, O Lord. All day long, I stretch
my hand toward You in prayer.

Do You work miracles for the dead?

Will the spirits of the deceased arise
with thanks to You?

Will anyone in Sheol tell of Your mercy
or anyone in Abaddon tell of Your faithful ways?

Will people who dwell in dark places
know about Your miracles or righteousness?

To You I cry for help, O Lord. Each morning,
my prayers enter Your presence.

Psalm 89:1-2, 5-17 – a prayer of Ethan

I will sing of the Lord's mercies forever!

I will proclaim Your faithfulness to all generations,
for Your unfailing love will last forever,
and the heavens establish Your faithfulness.

Every part of heaven will praise Your wonders,
Your greatness, Lord, and Your holy ones
will praise You for Your faithfulness, for who
in the heavens can compare to You?

The mightiest angels are not like You,
but the highest heavenly hosts stand in awe,
for You, God, are far more awe-inspiring than all
who surround Your throne.

O Lord, Commander of Heaven's Armies,
where is anyone as mighty as You?

You are wholly faithful, O Lord, and You rule
the oceans and subdue their waves.

You can overpower the greatest monsters
and scatter foes with Your mighty arm.

The heavens belong to You, and so does
the earth, for everything in the cosmos is Yours;
You created it all!

You formed it all – north to south, mountain
to mountain – and all will praise Your Name.

How powerful Your arm! How strong Your hand!
What glorious strength You have!
Your throne rests on righteousness and justice.

Mercy and truth stand, attentively, before You.

*How happy are those who hear a joyful call
to worship You, for they will walk in the light
of Your presence.*

*Day by day, they will rejoice in Your wonderful
reputation, Lord, and exult in Your righteousness,
for they find their strength in You.*

It pleases You to make us strong.

Psalm 89:38-52 – a prayer of Ethan

Have You rejected Your anointed one
and cast him angrily away?
Have You renounced Your covenant
and thrown down the crown You gave?
Have You torn down walls of protection
and ruined the defense of every fort?
Everyone passing by Your anointed
robs them and makes jokes!

Enemies grow stronger and rejoice!
You have made the sword of the anointed
lose its edge. You have refused to help
in the battle. You have ended splendor
and up-ended the throne! You have ended
the energy of Your anointed and poured
out public disgrace.

O, Lord, how long will this continue?
Will You hide Yourself forever?
How long will Your anger burn like fire?
Remember? My life is short, and sometimes
my very existence seems empty and futile.
No one lives forever. All die, and none can
escape the power of the grave.

Does Your love continue, Lord? Do Your
pledges to Your people go on, faithfully?
Then think about how Your servants are
disgraced – how my heart carries many
insults and mockeries from Your enemies.
Nevertheless, Lord, I will praise You –
forever and ever. Amen.

Psalm 90:1-4, 12-17 – a prayer of Moses

From generation to generation, Lord,
You have given us refuge.
Before You gave birth to the mountains,
the earth, the world –
            from eternity to eternity –
You are God.

When You say, "Return, descendants
of Adam," people return to dust,
for in Your sight a thousand years
pass by like yesterday –
like mere hours in a night.

Teach us to number our days with care,
so our hearts will develop with wisdom.

But, how long, Lord, before You turn to us,
Your servants, with compassion?

May Your faithful love assure us
each morning, so we may shout
with joy and gladness all our lives.

May we rejoice for as many days
as You have humbled us – for as many
years as we have seen adversity.

Let Your servants see Your work,
and our children see Your splendor!

Let Your favor, O Lord, our God, be on us,
and establish for us the work of our hands.
Yes, establish the work of our hands!

Psalm 92:4-5, 8 – a prayer of God's people

Lord, You make us so happy
by Your works,
we just want to sing for joy!

What great things You have done –
even when Your thoughts
and reasons are too deep
to understand!

You, O Lord, are Most High!
May You be honored forever.

Psalm 94:17-19 – a prayer of God's people

Unless You had been my help, Lord,
my soul would have lived in silence.

When I thought my foot slipped....
When I thought I was falling,
Your steady love,
Your unswerving mercy
held me up.

When I get anxious or
worried or upset,
You comfort my heart.
You console my soul.

Psalm 100 – a prayer of God's people

*Earth, I'm calling on you to make
a joyful noise to the Lord!*

*We worship You, Lord, with gladness.
We sing our way into Your presence.*

*We know You are God, and it is You,
Who has made us – we, Your people,
the sheep of Your pastures.*

*With thanks, we enter Your gates
and come into Your courts with praise.*

*We're so grateful to You,
we bless and hallow Your Name.*

*How good You are, Lord! How faithful!
Your mercy lasts forever, and Your truth
goes on and on to all generations.*

Psalm 102:1-12 – a prayer of a person who's suffering

Hear my prayer, O Lord!
Let my cry for help come to You.

Don't hide from me in the day
of my distress.

Incline Your ear to listen to me.
In the day I call, quickly answer,
for my days go up in smoke,
and my bones feel
as scorched as a hearth!

My smitten heart feels like
withering grass, and I forget
to eat.

Loudly I groan,
for my bones cling to my flesh.

I'm like a pelican in the wilderness,
an owl in waste places,

a lonely bird on a rooftop
as I lie awake.

People reproach me all day long!

Those who deride me use my name
as a curse!

My mouth fills with ashes
instead of bread,
and tears water my drink.
Your indignation and wrath
lift me up then cast me away!

My days become mere shadows,
and I wither like the grass,

but You, O Lord,
live forever!

Your Name remains for all generations.

Psalm 102:13-14, 25-28 – a prayer of a person who's suffering

Arise with compassion for Your people,
for the time has come to be gracious!
The appointed time has come.

Surely Your servants will find pleasure
amidst the ruins and feel compassion
for the very dust.

Long ago, You founded the earth and
made the heavens the work of Your hands.
Yet they will perish, but You will endure.

All creation will wear out like a garment,
but, like clothing, You will change them,
and they will be changed!

You, however, are the same.
Your years never end.

May the children of Your servants continue too.
May our children's children be recognized before You.

Psalm 103:1-6 – a prayer of David

Bless the Lord, O my soul
and all that is within me
bless His holy Name.

Bless the Lord, O my soul
and forget not all God's benefits

For, You, O Lord, forgive our sins
and heal us
of whatever robs us of ease.

You save us from a low-life
and bless us with love and mercy.

You fill our lives with good things
and make us feel as strong
as a young eagle.

Psalm 104:1-5, 24, 30 – a prayer of David

O, Lord, my God, how great You are!

Honor and majesty clothe You,
and light covers You like a garment.
You stretch out the heavens like a tent.

You build chambers on the water.
Clouds form Your chariot as You ride
on the wings of the wind.

You send the wind as Your messenger,
and fire and flames as Your ministers.
You establish the earth soundly
on foundations that do not fail.

O, Lord, how diverse are Your works!
You formed the world in Your wisdom!

When You send forth Your Spirit,
we are created, and You renew
the face of the earth.

Psalm 106:47 – a prayer of God's people

O Lord, our God, rescue us.

Gather us together,
so we may give thanks
to Your holy Name.

May we glory
in Your praise.

Psalm 108:1-6 – a prayer of David

What confidence my heart has in You, O God!
No wonder I can sing Your praises
with my whole heart!

Wake up, lyre and harp!
I will awaken the dawn with my song.

I will thank You, Lord, among all the people.
I will sing Your praises among the nations.

Higher than the heavens is Your unfailing love!
Your faithfulness reaches the clouds.

Be exalted, O God, above the highest heavens!
May Your glory shine over all the earth.

Please rescue Your beloved people now!
Answer us. Save us by Your power.

Psalm 109:1-4, 21-31 – a prayer of David

Lord God Whom I praise, do not be silent!

Hate-filled, deceit-filled mouths speak against me
with lying tongues.

Hateful words surround me, attacking without cause.
In return for my love, I receive accusations
even though I keep on praying.

But You, Lord God, deal kindly with me
because of Your Name.
The goodness of Your steadfast love delivers me.

I am in trouble, in need.

My heart is wounded.

I fade like an evening shadow.
I'm shaken off like a locust.

My knees quiver from fasting.
My body shrinks.

I'm an object of ridicule.
My accusers see me and shake their heads in scorn.

Help me, my Lord, my God!

Save me according to Your unswerving love,
so everyone will know this is Your hand, Lord,
and You have done it.

Even if people curse me, I know You will bless.

When they rise up, they'll be ashamed,

but Your servant will have cause for joy.
Disgrace will clothe my accusers,
and shame will cover them like a cloak.

Lord, I will fervently,
passionately,
enthusiastically
thank You aloud,
praising You in the presence of many,
for You stand at the hand of those in need
and save us from condemnation.

Psalm 118:1-6, 19-28 – a prayer of God's people

Give thanks for the Lord is good!
Your loving kindness lasts forever.

Oh, let God's people say:
The Lord's loving kindness lasts forever.

Oh, let every congregation say:
The Lord's loving kindness lasts forever.

Oh, let everyone in awe of God say:
The Lord's loving kindness lasts forever.

In my distress, I called on You, Lord,
and You answered me and set me
in a goodly place.

The Lord is for me! I have no need to fear.
What can people do to me?

Open Your gates of righteousness,
and I shall enter with thanks to You, Lord.

Here's the gate of the Lord!
The upright enter through it.

I give thanks to You, Lord, for You have
answered me and become my salvation.

The stone which the builders rejected
has become the chief cornerstone!

This is Your doing, Lord,
and it is marvelous in our eyes.

This is the day You have made.

Let us rejoice and be glad in it!

Save us, O Lord, we pray!
O Lord, we ask You to send us success.

Blessed is the one who comes
in the Name of the Lord –
blessed from the house of the Lord.

You, O Lord God, have given us light.
You are my God, and I will give You thanks.
You are my God, and I will exalt You.

Psalm 119:1-14 – a prayer of God's people

How blessed are those who live with integrity,
who follow Your teachings, Lord.
How blessed are those who obey Your written word.

Wholeheartedly they search for You.
They do nothing wrong when they follow Your directions.
You have commanded us to follow Your guidance carefully.
I pray my ways may become firmly established,
so I can obey Your laws.

I never feel ashamed when I study Your word.
I give thanks to You as I learn Your righteous regulations.
I want to obey Your laws, Lord. Never leave me alone!

When young people want to live a pure life,
they do it by holding onto Your word.

Wholeheartedly I searched for You.
Don't let me stray away from Your commandments!

I treasure Your promises within me, so I won't sin
against You.

Thanks to You, O Lord, I've learned Your laws.

My lips have repeated each regulation that comes
from Your lips.

What joy I find in the way shown by Your written word –
more joy than can be found in all kinds of riches!

Psalm 119:15-27 – a prayer of God's people

Lord, I want to think about Your guidance and values
as I study Your ways.
Your laws make me happy, and I won't forget
what You have said.

Be kind to me as I live, holding onto Your word.
Uncover my eyes, so I can see everything miraculous
in Your teachings.

I feel like a foreigner in the world.
Don't hide Your decrees from me!

My very soul longs endlessly for Your regulations,
but You warn pride-filled people, who wander away
from Your commandments into areas of condemnation.

Remove the contempt and insults that have fallen on me,
for I have obeyed Your written word.

When influential people plot against me,
I consider what You might want me to do.
Indeed, Your written word makes me happy.
Your words are my best friends!

I'm getting closer to death now,
but I pray for the new life You have promised.
I admitted what I've done, and You answered me.

Teach me Your laws,
so I may reflect on Your miracles.

Psalm 119:28-37 – a prayer of God's people

My tears are drowning me, Lord!
Give me the strength You promised.

Turn me from lives of lies,
and grace me with Your teachings.

I choose a life of faithfulness to You,
and I set Your regulations before me.

Tightly, I cling to Your written word!
O Lord, let me not be put to shame!

Eagerly, I pursue Your commandments
as You continue to expand my understanding.

O Lord, teach me to live by Your laws,
and obey them to the end.

Help me, too, to comprehend Your teachings,
so I can follow and guard them with all my heart.

Lead me on the path Your commandments take,
for I am happy to follow.

Direct my heart toward Your written word
and away from underhanded acts or choices.

Turn my eyes from anything worthless,
and renew my life in Your ways.

Psalm 119:38-47 – a prayer of God's people

Keep Your promises to me –
Your devoted servant in awe of You.

Turn away the disgrace I dread,
for Your judgment is good.

How I long for Your precepts!
Revive my life with Your righteousness.

Let Your blessings reach me, O Lord.
Rescue me as You have promised,
then I can answer those who insult me,
for I trust You mean what You say.

Do not take a single word of truth
from my mouth, for I hope
in Your judgments.

I want to follow Your teachings
forever and ever.
Then I can walk around freely,
knowing I sought Your guidance.

In the presence of famous people –
even royalty – I will talk about
Your written word without shame.

Your commandments, which I love,
fill me with delight.

Psalm 119:48-59 – a prayer of God's people

Lord, I lift my hands to You in prayer
because I love Your high standards
as I meditate on Your laws.

Remembering the word You gave me
gives me hope and comfort – even in misery.
Your promises renew my life.

Prideful people have cruelly mocked me,
but I have not turned my back on Your teachings.

I remembered Your standards set long ago
and took comfort in them, but
hateful people who abandon Your teachings
get me hot with anger!

To me, Your laws are like lyrics to sing
in this place where I don't fit in.

At night I think about Your Name, O Lord,
and I remember what You've taught,
for I aim to obey Your guiding principles.

You are my inheritance, Lord,
and I promise to hold onto Your word.

With all my heart, I want Your favor
and the kindness You have promised.

Psalm 119:59-72 – a prayer of God's people

Thinking back on my life, I've kept my feet
aimed toward Your written instructions,
and, with no hesitation, I hurry
to obey Your commands.

Sometimes I sense wickedness around me
hindering my steps, but I won't forget Your teaching.

In the middle of the night, I awake to thank You
for Your righteous rules and regulations.

I am a friend to everyone who fears You –
to everyone who follows Your ways.

O Lord, Your mercy fills the earth!
Teach me Your laws.

You have treated me well, O Lord,
just as You promised.

Now, help me to use good judgment
in applying my knowledge of You,
for I truly believe in Your ways.

Before, when You let me suffer,
I wandered away from You, but now
I hold onto Your word to steady me.

How good You are! You do good too!
Teach me Your standards.

Some people have arrogantly smeared me
with lies, but I obey Your truths with all my heart.
Their hearts seem cold and insensitive,
but I am warmed by Your teachings.

My suffering served a good purpose,
for it gave me time to learn what You want.

Every teaching, every word You speak
is more priceless than thousands
of pieces of silver and gold.

Psalm 119:73-80 – a prayer of God's people

You created me with Your own hands, Lord!
You made me who I am.

Help me to understand what that means
as I learn Your commandments.

Let those who fear You look at me with joy,
for I base my hope on Your word.

I know Your rulings are just and fair, O Lord,
and You were right to let me suffer.

Now, let Your mercy comfort me as You
have promised.

Let Your compassion cover me, so I may live,
for Your teachings bless me.

Let prideful people be ashamed of lying
when I reflect on Your ways.

Let those who are in awe of You turn to me,
so we can talk about Your written word.

Let my heart be filled with integrity
regarding Your laws, so I won't be disgraced.

Psalm 119:81-96 – a prayer of God's people

Lord, my soul – my whole self – feels weak from waiting
for You to save me
as I base my hope on Your word.

I have eye-strain from looking for evidence of Your promises
and I cannot help but ask, "When will You comfort me?"

Sometimes I feel as shriveled up and dried out as old leather,
but I have not forgotten Your ways.

What's left of my life?
Will those who bully me be brought to justice?

Pride-filled people dig pits to trap me and defy
Your teachings.

I know Your ways can be trusted, but some people
pester and persecute me with lies! Help me, Lord!

They've almost wiped me out,
but I'm hanging onto Your guiding principles.

Renew me with Your mercy,
so I can obey Your instructions to me.

Your word, O Lord, is established in heaven forever.
Your faithfulness endures from generation to generation.

You set the earth in place, and it stands.

All things are able to stand because of Your laws,
which are Your servants.

If Your teachings had saddened me, I would have died
in this miserable time,

but I won't forget Your guiding principles,
for they renewed my life.

I am Yours.

Save me.

I search for Your way.

Wicked ones wait to destroy me,
but I want to hear what You have to say.

Everything has its limits,
but not Your word – Your eternal word.

Psalm 119:97-105 – a prayer of God's people

Oh, how I love Your teachings!
I think about them all day.

Your commandments make me wiser
than my opponents,
because Your word is always with me.

With Your written instructions in my thoughts,
I have more insight than my teachers!
I have more wisdom than those with years
of experience, because I have Your principles
to guide me.

Just wanting to obey Your word
keeps me from paths of evil.
I have not neglected the regulations
You've taught.

How sweet are Your promises –
sweeter than honey!

As Your principles guide me, I gain
understanding,
but I hate ways that lead to lies.

Your word is a lamp for my feet –
a light on the path to You.

Psalm 119:106-111 – a prayer of God's people

I made a promise, and I'll keep it.
I promised to follow Your regulations,
which arise from Your righteousness.

I've suffered, O Lord, but You
renewed my life as You promised.

Please accept my praise, O Lord,
which I gladly give for Your teachings.

Even if I take my life into my own hands,
I won't forget what You've taught me.

Impious people have set traps for me,
but I haven't wandered away from
Your ways that guide me.

Your written word is mine forever!
Your word is the joy of my heart.

Psalm 119:112-125 – a prayer of God's people

My decision to obey Your laws
offers a reward that never ends!

I do not like deceitful people,
but I love Your teachings, Lord.

You are my hiding place and my shield.
I base my hopes on what You say.

Anyone who wants to do wrong
can stay away from me,
for I want to obey You, God.

Help me, God, as You have promised,
so I may have life.

Don't let my hope be disappointed.

Hold me, and I will be safe
and will always respect Your laws.

Lies mislead! But people feel
Your rejection when they've wandered
away from You.

Get rid of wickedness! It's rubbish!
Your written word, though, is to love.

My whole body trembles in awe of You,
and sometimes I'm afraid of Your laws!

I try to do what's fair and right, so please,
don't leave me at the mercy of oppressors.

My well-being needs Your assurance.

*Oh, don't let "superior" people
put me down!*

*I have eye-strain from looking for You
to save me – from looking
for the fulfillment of Your promises.*

*Kindly treat me, and teach me Your ways,
for I am here to serve You.*

*Help me to understand and know
Your word more fully.*

Psalm 119:126-132 – a prayer of God's people

I need You to act now, Lord!

Other people have done away with Your teachings,
but I love Your word more than gold –
more than the purest, finest gold!

I want to walk in line with Your guiding principles,
for I hate every pathway leading to lies.

Your written words are like a miracle to me,
so, of course, I want to obey them!

Your word is like a door opened to the light,
so even an inexperienced person can understand.

Sometimes I feel as if I'm panting and drooling
for Your word, Your guidance!

Turn Your mercy toward me, Lord,
as You vowed to do for those who love Your Name.

Psalm 119:133-143 – a prayer of God's people

Your promises secure my steps, Lord.
Let nothing else control me!
Save me from oppressive people,
and help me to obey Your word.
Look upon me favorably,
and teach me Your laws.

My eyes pour out torrents of tears
over those who don't follow Your teachings.

You're blameless, O Lord,
and Your regulations are fair to all.
You have given us Your instructions
in writings – just, fair, and dependable.

I'm devoted completely to Your words,
which those who go against me forgot.
Your promises, which I love,
can bear up to thorough scrutiny.

I have no importance or honor on my own,
but I'll never forget Your guidance.
Your righteousness is eternal,
and Your teachings trustworthy.

Even when trouble and hardships find me,
Your commandments cheer me up.

Psalm 119:144-159 – a prayer of God's people

Your written word is exactly right!
Help me to understand what You say, so I can live it.

When I call You with all my heart, please answer me, Lord.
I want to obey Your word, and I have called out to You.

Rescue me from getting off track.
Help me to obey the instructions You've given.

Before morning light, I cry out for Your help,
for my hope resides in Your word.

At night, my eyes stay open as I reflect on Your word,
and I count on Your mercy to respond to me.

Revive my life, O Lord, in accordance with Your regulations.

People who plot against me draw near me
but go far from Your teachings.

You are near me, Lord, and I count on Your word!

Long ago, I learned from scripture
that You made Your word to last forever,
but see? I'm feeling low and in need of Your salvation
even though I've never forgotten Your teachings.

Plead my case for me! Save me! Give me
the new life You promised.

Some people stay away from Your word.

They haven't searched Your governing principles,
even though Your acts of compassion are too many
to count, O Lord.

Give me a new life, guided by Your regulations.
Many oppose me – even persecute me, but
I haven't turned away from Your written word.

I hate how people betray You when they don't
believe Your promises!

See how I love Your guiding principles, O Lord?
In keeping with Your mercy, give me a new kind of life.

Psalm 119:160-165 – a prayer of God's people

Only the truth resides in Your word.
Every word of Your righteousness endures forever.

Powerful people have put me down for no reason,
but only Your words of truth fill my heart with awe!

I find joy in Your promises –
like the joy of finding a priceless treasure.

Lies disgust me!
But I love the truth of Your teachings.

I'd like to praise You at least seven times a day
for giving me Your guidance on how to live upright.

What lasting peace comes to those who love
Your teachings!

Then nothing can make Your people stumble.

Psalm 119:166-176 – a prayer of God's people

O Lord, I'm waiting and hoping
for You to rescue me!

I've followed Your commandments
and obeyed Your written instructions,
for I very much love Your word.
I've followed Your guiding principles
and Your written word, while
laying my whole life before You.

Let my cry for help come before You, O Lord.
Help me to get clear about Your promises.
Let my pleas for mercy come before You.
Liberate me as You promised!

Let my lips gush with praises
as You teach me Your ways.
Let my tongue sing of Your promises,
knowing all of Your laws are fair and just.

Let Your mighty hand help me,
because I've chosen to follow Your guidance.
I long for You to liberate me, O Lord,
for Your teachings make me happily hope.

Let my soul be renewed, so I can praise You.
Let Your guiding principles assist me,
but if I wander away like a lost lamb, Lord,
search for me,
for I never want to forget Your commandments.

Psalm 120:1-2 – a prayer of God's people

To You, Lord, I took my troubles.

To You, I cried out,
and You answered my prayer.

Save me, O Lord,
from untruthful people
and all who deceive.

Psalm 123 – a prayer of God's people

I look up to You –
the One Who sits enthroned in heaven.

As servants depend on their masters
and maids on their mistresses,
so we depend on the Lord our God
to take pity on us.

Show us Your mercy, O Lord.

Show us Your mercy,
for we have suffered more than our share
of contempt.

We have suffered more than our share
of ridicule from those who are careless.

We have suffered more than our share
of contempt from the arrogant.

Psalm 125:4-5 – a prayer of God's people

O Lord, do good
to those who try to do right –
to those with decent motives.

When people become crooked,
lead them away
with other troublemakers.

Let there be peace
among Your people.

Psalm 130:1-6 – a prayer of God's people

Out of the depths, I cry to You, O Lord.
Let Your ear be attentive to my voice.

If You were to keep records of all our
wrongdoings, who could stand?
But with You is forgiveness!
So we revere You.

I'm waiting for You, Lord.
My whole soul waits!
More than watchmen for the morning....
More than watchmen for the morning....

Psalm 131:1-2 – a prayer of David

Lord, I don't want to be haughty!

*I don't want to see myself
as better than anyone else.*

*I don't want to occupy myself
with things too much for me –
things over my head.*

In You, I am calm.

*My soul quiets down
like a weaned child in motherly arms.*

Psalm 132:8-9 – a prayer of God's people

Arise, O Lord!
Come to Your place of rest
with the ark of Your power.

Clothe Your priests
with righteousness.

Let Your godly ones
sing with joy.

Psalm 138:1-3, 7,8 – a prayer of David

I praise You, Lord, with my whole heart.
Even if there were another god,
I would sing Your praise.

I bow before You.
I praise Your Name.

You are loving, steadfast, and kind.
You are truth.
But Your Name is higher than anything!

When I cry out to You,
You answer me and give me
the strength I need.

Even if I'm walking into trouble,
You reach out to me.
You stretch out Your hand to save me.

Psalm 139:1-12 – a prayer of David

O Lord, You have searched me and known me!
You know when I sit down and when I get up.
You understand my thoughts from afar.
You examine my comings and goings and lying down,
and You're intimately acquainted with all my ways.
Even before I know what I'm going to say,
behold, You, O Lord, know every word!

You've enclosed me behind and before
and laid Your hand upon me.
Such knowledge is too wonderful for me –
so high, I cannot attain it.

Where can I go from Your Spirit?
Where can I flee from Your presence?

If I ascend into heaven, You are there.
If I make my bed in deepest darkness,
behold, You are there!

If I take the wings of the dawn
or dwell in the remotest part of the sea,
Your hand will lead me.
Your right hand will hold me.

If I say, "Surely, the darkness will overwhelm me
and the light around me be as night,"
even the darkest darkness is not dark to You!
The night is as bright as day,
for to You, darkness and light are both alike.

Psalm 139:13-24 – a prayer of David

Lord, You formed my inward parts.
You wove me in my mother's womb!

I give thanks to You, for I am
fearfully and wonderfully made.

Your works fill me with wonder,
and my very soul knows that quite well.

My frame was never hidden from You
when I came together in secret – as though
skillfully wrought in the depths of the earth.

Your eyes have seen my embryonic self,
and in Your book You have written
all the days ordained for me – even before
my day of birth had yet begun.

How precious are Your thoughts, O God!
How vast the sum of them!

If I tried to count them, it'd be like trying
to count each particle of sand.

When I'm awake, I'm with You, but oh, I wish
You'd get rid of malice and hatefulness!

I wish violent people would stay far from me,
for they say terrible things about You,
and Your enemies take Your Name in vain.

I do not like anyone who hates You, Lord!
I loathe those who speak out against You.
I hate their actions with the highest hatred,
and they have become my enemies too.

Search me, O God, and know my heart.

Test me to know my anxious thoughts, and see if there's anything hateful or hurtful in me.

Lead me in Your everlasting way.

Psalm 140:1, 7 – a prayer of David

Deliver me from evil, Lord!
Protect me from violence.

O Lord, my God,
my mighty Savior,
You have covered
my head for the battle.

Psalm 141:1-3 – a prayer of David

I'm calling to You, Lord.
Please hurry and help!

Let my prayers come before You
like incense.

Let the lifting of my hands
be like an evening sacrifice.

Let my words be under
Your control.

Be the doorkeeper of my lips.

Psalm 143:1, 7-8 – a prayer of David

Hear my prayer, O Lord.
Bring Your ear close.
Answer me in Your righteousness,
Your faithfulness.

Answer me quickly,
for my spirit languishes!
If You hide Your face from me,
I'd be in the dark – in a pit!

Let me hear Your loving kindness
in the morning, Lord,
for I trust – oh, I trust –
in You!

Teach me the way in which
I should walk, for to You
I lift up my soul, my life.
For to You, I lift up my soul.

Psalm 144 – a prayer of David

How blessed You are, my Lord, my Rock,
for You prepare me for every conflict
and strengthen me to take on whatever comes.

You are my fortress – loving and kind,
my stronghold and my deliverer, my shield,
and the One in Whom I take refuge
as You subdue everyone who's against me.

O, Lord, who are we that You
take note of us?

What is humankind that You
give us any thought?

We're like a mere breath
with our days like a passing shadow.

Come down from Your heavens, O Lord.
Touch the mountains. Flash forth lightning.

Scatter Your enemies. Send out arrows
and confuse them.

Stretch forth Your hand from on high.

Rescue me! Deliver me from deep waters,
from the hands of deceitful people.
I don't know them or why they do what they do!

To You, I'll sing a new song, O God.

With stringed instruments, I'll sing praises to You –
Savior of leaders,
Rescuer of Your servants.

Rescue me now! Deliver me from the hands
of deceitful people, who behave falsely,
but let our young people be like growing plants,
like beautiful pillars fashioned for a palace.

Give us a plentiful harvest with every kind of produce.
Let our flocks multiple and cover our fields.
Let our cattle be healthy and free of mishaps.
Let there be no reason to cry in the streets!

How blessed are Your people!
How blessed are those whose God is You, Lord!

Psalm 150 – a prayer of God's people

Praise the Lord!

Lord, we praise You in the sanctuary.
We praise You to the highest heavens.

We praise You for Your mighty acts.
We praise You for Your greatness.

We praise You with melodies –
with song and dance.

We praise You with instruments
of music.

May everything that has breath –
everything that can make a sound –
praise You.

Praise the Lord.

Isaiah 6:5 – a prayer of Isaiah

It's no use! It's over!
I'm doomed!

I'm so sinful,
even my lips are filthy,
and I live among
such foul-mouthed people!

And yet, somehow
my eyes have recognized
You, the King –
You, the Lord of Hosts,
You, the Commander
of Heaven's Armies.

Jeremiah 10:23-25 – a prayer of Jeremiah

Yes, I know, Lord.
Our lives don't belong only to ourselves.
We can't even plan our own best course.

Correct me, Lord, but please
be gentle about it!
If You get too angry with me, I'd want to die!

Instead, pour Your wrath
on nations that refuse to acknowledge You –
on people who do not call on Your Name.

Such people have been devouring us!
Such people have created such waste!

Jeremiah 12:1-4 – a prayer of Jeremiah

When I present my side of things to You,
You're always right!

And yet, I want to ask about Your idea of justice.
Like, why do terrible people succeed?
Why do deceitful, disloyal, double-dealing people
have peace and quiet in their lives?

You plant.
They take root.
They grow and produce fruit.
They speak nicely about You,
but their hearts are far from You, Lord!

You know me, O Lord.
You recognize me and my devotion toward You.
So how about if you drag away
treacherous people like livestock to be slaughtered
and prepare their wrongdoings to die?

How long will the land itself cry out to You, Lord?
How long will plants and crops dry up and wither?

The animals, the birds are dying!
Why? Because some people are cruel, and they think
You have no clue what they are doing.

Jeremiah 14:7-9 – a prayer of Jeremiah

Do something, Lord!
Think of Your reputation!

Even though our sins speak against us –
even though we've been unfaithful
and have wronged You,
You are still our hope!

You are The One Who saves us
in times of trouble.

Don't be a stranger to us, Lord.

Don't be like a visitor who only stays
for one night.

And don't be taken by surprise –
like some muscle-bound guy who suddenly
realizes he can do nothing to help!

You, O Lord, are with us.

We're called by Your Name.
Please do not abandon us.

Jeremiah 14:20-22 – a prayer of Jeremiah

We confess!

We've acted badly, Lord,
and so have our ancestors.

Our whole family has sinned against You,
and yet, surely
Your character will not allow You
to abandon us, Lord,
nor disgrace Your glorious throne.

Please remember Your promises to us
for we rely on You.

What worthless foreign god could
send us rain?

The sky needs You
to do such things, O Lord our God.
And so,
we wait for You to help.

Jeremiah 15:15-18 – a prayer of Jeremiah

*O Lord, You understand me! You
remember me. You take care of me.
You deal with people who treat me badly.*

*Be patient with me, and keep me close,
but I need to let You know I'm being
insulted because of You.*

*When I found Your words, I ate them up!
What joy! What delight I have, O Lord,
God of Heavenly Hosts
because I am called by Your Name!*

*If someone mocks or scoffs at me,
I don't hang around, waiting for more –
even if it means being alone –
for I know Your hand is on me.*

*You filled me with indignation over wrongs,
but it feels like I myself am wrought
with an incurable wound that refuses to heal.*

*Oh, please, don't let me down! Don't be to me
like a stream of water, drying in summer heat.*

Jeremiah 17:13-17 – a prayer of Jeremiah

Lord God and hope of Your people,
whoever abandons You will be put to shame!

All who turn away from You will find their whole lives
written only in dust,
for they have abandoned You and Your fountain
of living water.

Heal me, Lord, and I will be healed.

Save me, and I will be saved,
for You alone are my praise.

Do You hear people taunting me, asking
"Where is the word of the Lord? Let it come!"
And yet, I have not run away from the work
You have given me nor longed for disaster to fall.
You've heard my words, spoken in Your presence.

Please don't terrorize me – ever,
for You alone are my refuge in troubled times.

Jeremiah 20:7-12 – a prayer of Jeremiah

O Lord, You deceived me, and I was deceived!
You overpowered me and won.

(I did not think that following You would be like this!)

All day, people make fun of me and mock.
No wonder, because whenever I speak
what You have given me to say, I have to shout:
"Violence! Destruction!"

Day after day, Your word has made me
the object of insults and contempt.

So I started telling myself, "I'm going to forget You,
Lord, and not even mention Your Name."

But then,
Your word became like fire shut up in my bones
until I could hold it in no longer!

People keep saying, "Terror abounds!
Let's report him. Just report him!"

And even my closest friends seem to wait
and want to see me stumble. They say,
"Maybe he'll be tricked, and then we
can overpower him and get revenge!"

Lord, You're on my side
like a terrifying warrior!
Whoever persecutes me
will surely be the one to stumble.

They cannot win! And when they don't succeed,
they'll be ashamed with unforgettable shame.

*Lord of Heaven's Warriors, You investigate
the righteous and see each thought and motive.*

*I wish You'd take revenge on them
for I'm bringing my case to You.*

Jeremiah 32:17-20 – a prayer of Jeremiah

O Lord Most High, Supreme Ruler,
Your strength and power made
the heavens and the earth.

Nothing is too hard for You!

You show Your unfailing love and mercy
to thousands of generations, but
You also bring the effects of one
generation's sin upon the next.

Great and powerful God –
Lord of Heaven's Armies
You have total wisdom and do great
and mighty miracles.
You see how people act and give them
what they deserve.

The miraculous signs and wonders You did
in the land of our slave-masters are still
remembered to this day! And You have
continued to do wonders around the world,
making Your Name famous.

Lamentations 1:20-22 – a prayer of God's people

Lord, I'm in such distress
my insides are churning!

My heart breaks,
for I've been rebellious against You.

In the streets, swords take the children.
Inside, death occurs.

People have heard my groaning,
but no one comforts me.

My enemies hear of my misfortune,
but they gladly think You caused it.

Bring on the day You warned them about,
so they'll be as miserable as I am!

Let their wickedness come before You.
Then deal with them as they have dealt with me.

But, because of my own misdoings,
groans fill me,
and my heart is sick.

Lamentations 3:55-64 – a prayer of God's people

Out of the lowest pit, I call on Your Name, O Lord,
and You have heard my voice.

Don't conceal Your ears from my prayer, my cry for help!

When I called on You, You told me, "Do not be afraid."

You stood up for me, O Lord, and pleaded my cause.

You've redeemed my life.

You've seen how I've been oppressed.

O, Lord, judge my case.

You've seen their vengeance and schemes against me.
You have heard their reproach, O Lord, and their plots!

My attackers whisper against me all day long.

Can You see them sitting around or standing up
to mock me?

Will You repay them, O Lord, in accordance with the work
of their hands?

Lamentations 5:1-5, 19-21 – a prayer of God's people

Lord, do You remember
what has happened to us?
Can You see how disgraced
we have been?

Strangers
have our inheritance,
foreigners our homes.
We are orphaned
and fatherless.
Our mothers are widows.

We have to pay
for water to drink,
and firewood costs too much!
People who pursue us
close in on our heels.

We're so tired, Lord,
and we have no rest.
But, You, Lord, remain
the same forever.

From generation to generation,
You remain on Your throne,
and yet You keep forgetting us.
Why have You let us go for so long?

Restore us, O Lord!
Bring us back to You!
Give us the joy we once had.

Daniel 9:4-9 – a prayer of Daniel

Lord, You are great –
the only God –
and You deserve great honor.

You keep Your promises.
You show mercy to those who love You
and obey Your commands.

But we have sinned.
We've done wrong!
We've acted wickedly.
We've rebelled against You.

We haven't listened to Your servants –
the prophets, who spoke to rulers,
leaders, ancestors, and all people
in Your Name.

You are righteous, Lord, but we –
Your people, whom You have scattered
in countries far and near –
are ashamed of our sins.

And yet, even though we broke faith
with You, O Lord, our God,
You remain compassionate and forgiving.

Daniel 9:10-15 – a prayer of Daniel

Lord, when You gave us Your teachings
through Your servants and prophets,
I'm sorry to say, we didn't listen.

We didn't obey.

All of us have ignored what You taught!
All of us have closed our ears!

And so, You let fall on us
the curses You'd warned us about –
the curses Moses recorded in the Torah.

We sinned against You.

So You did exactly what You said You'd do
to us and our rulers by letting disasters
fall!

Nowhere on earth has anything happened
to other people as it has to Your children!

What disasters – exactly as You warned!

And yet, we don't seem to try to regain Your favor
by turning our backs on wrongs and facing truth.

You had to do what You did, Lord God,
for You are just and right in all You do.

We just didn't listen to You!

Daniel 9:17-19 – a prayer of Daniel

Our God, hear my prayer.
Listen to my request.

For Your own sake, Lord,
look with favor on Your
holy place, lying now in ruins!

Open Your ears and listen,
my God.

Open Your eyes and see
ruin in the city called
by Your Name.

We don't make this request
because we deserve it,
but because You are filled
with compassion.

Listen to us, Lord.
Forgive us, Lord.
Pay attention, and act
without further delay!

Do this for Your sake,
my God, because this place
and Your people are called
by Your Name.

Jonah 1:14 – a prayer of Jonah

Earnestly, we pray to You, O Lord.

*Do not let us perish because of what
other people have done wrong!*

*Do not hold us accountable
for innocent blood!*

But You, O Lord, can do as You please.

Jonah 2:2-9 – a prayer of Jonah

I called to You, Lord, in my distress,
and You answered me!
From the belly of death, I cried for help,
and You heard me!

When You tossed me into the depths
of the sea, the waters overcame me.
Billows and breakers swept over me,
and I said, "I've been banished
from Your sight!" I wondered if I
would ever see Your holy sanctuary again.

Water engulfed me, and I sank into the sea.
Seaweed wrapped around my head.
I sank to the sea-roots of mountains.
Around me, the earth
closed like prison bars,
but You raised me
from this sinkhole,
O Lord, my God!

As my life faded away,
I remembered You.
My prayer floated up to You,
reaching Your holy presence.
Worshippers of worthless things
forsake Your faithful love, but I
will give You my voice
in a sacrifice of thanksgiving.
I'll do as I promised, Lord,
for You alone hold my salvation.

Habakkuk 1:2-5 – a prayer of Habakkuk

How long, O Lord, must I cry for help
and You not listen?

How long must I call "Violence!"
and You not save?

Why have You made me sensitive
to injustice
when You tolerate those wrongs?

Oppression! Violence! Ongoing strife
confronts me, and conflicts escalate.

No wonder the law is ineffective!
Justice doesn't come into view.

Wicked people avert righteous responses,
perverting justice!

What do You want me to see?
When will You astonish me?

For You have promised
You're bringing about something
I won't believe even when I hear about it!

Habakkuk 1:12-13 – a prayer of Habakkuk

Haven't You
been around forever,
Almighty God?

You won't ever die,
my Holy Lord,
but You have
destined others
to be punished.

You're too pure
to watch wickedness,
and You can't tolerate
wrongdoing, so why
do You tolerate deceitful,
disloyal, double-crossing
ways some people behave?

Why do You keep silent
when maliciousness
swallows up
kindness and
decency?

Habakkuk 3:2 – a prayer of Habakkuk

I've heard all about You, Lord,
and I'm filled with awe over
Your amazing works!

In this time of deep need,
please help us again as you did
in years gone by.

Even in anger,
remember Your great mercy.

Habakkuk 3:8-16 – a prayer of Habakkuk

Did You strike the rivers and part the sea
in anger, Lord?

Did You act in annoyance? No!

You sent chariots of salvation to Your people!

You waved Your bow and showed a quiver
of arrows. You split rivers flowing on earth
as mountains watched and trembled.

Onward swept the raging sea!
The mighty waters cried out,
lifting their hands in submission.

The sun and moon stood still
as brilliant arrows flew forth,
and Your glittering spears
flashed across the sky.

Your anger marched across the land.
Your fury trampled nations.

In full force, You went forth
to rescue Your chosen people,
to save Your anointed children.

You crushed the head of evil then stripped
its bones from head to toe. You used
its own weapons against it, destroying
the chief, who rushed out like a whirlwind,
thinking Your people would be easy prey.

You trampled down the sea with Your horses,
and the mighty waters piled high on either side.

When I heard this, I trembled.
My lips quivered with fear.

My legs gave way beneath me,
and I shook in terror!

Now I'll wait quietly for a day to come when
You put a stop to those who invade us – now.

Habakkuk 3:17-19 – a prayer of Habakkuk

Even though the fig trees have no blossoms,
and no grapes huddle together on the vines....

Even though olive crops dry up,
and fields lie fruitless and empty....

Even though flocks die in the fields,
and the cattle barns stand empty,

yet I will rejoice in the Lord!
I will be joyful in the God of my salvation!

For You, Sovereign Lord, are my strength!

You make me as surefooted as a deer,
able to leap across high places.

Prayers from the New Testament

Matthew 6:9-13 – a prayer of Jesus

"Our Father which art in heaven,
Hallowed be thy name.
Thy kingdom come,
Thy will be done in earth,
as it is in heaven.

Give us this day our daily bread.
And forgive us our debts,
as we forgive our debtors.

And lead us not into temptation,
but deliver us from evil:

For thine is the kingdom,
and the power, and the glory,
for ever. Amen."

[Quoted from the *King James Version* of the Bible, *KJV.*]

Matthew 8:2 – a prayer of a leper

Lord,

if You
are willing,

You can
heal me

and make me
clean.

Matthew 8:8 – a prayer of a Roman officer

Lord, I am not worthy
to have You come under my roof,

but speak only a word,
and healing will happen!

Matthew 8:25 – a prayer of Jesus' followers

Lord!
Save us!

Do not let us
drown!

Matthew 11:25-26 – a prayer of Jesus

O Father, Lord of heaven and earth,
thank You for hiding Your wisdom
from those who think
they're clever and wise
but revealing Your insights
to childlike people.

Yes, Father!
What pleasure this brings!

Matthew 14:30 – a prayer of Peter

Lord, I'm frightened!

*I'm starting to sink
too low to keep my head up.*

Save me, Lord!

Matthew 17:15 – a prayer of a parent

*Lord, please have mercy
on my child,
who is suffering severely.*

*Let our children neither fall
nor drown.*

Matthew 20:30-33 – a prayer of blind men

Lord, Son of David,
have mercy on us!

Lord, Son of David,
have mercy on us!

Lord Jesus,
we want to see.

Matthew 26:39 – a prayer of Jesus

My Father,
if possible,
please

let this bitter cup
pass
from me.

Yet,
not as I will,
but as You will.

Matthew 27:46 – a prayer of Jesus

My God!
My God!
Why?

Have You
forsaken
me?

Luke 1:38 – a prayer of Mary

Here I am, Lord!

Let it be to me

as You have said.

Luke 1:46-50 – a prayer of Mary

With all my heart, I praise You, Lord!
What favor You have shown!

From now on, every generation
will call me blessed
because of the great things
You have done for me.

Holy is Your Name!

In every generation,
You give mercy upon mercy
to all who honor You.

Luke 1:68-70, 76, 77 – a prayer of Zechariah

Blessed are You, Lord God of Israel!
You have visited us and provided
redemption for Your people!
You have raised up a mighty Savior
from the house of David,
just as You promised ages ago
through the holy prophets.

And, now my child will be
a prophet of the Most High
to go before the Lord
and prepare the way
for You to give people
good news of salvation
as You forgive our sins.

Luke 2:29-32 – a prayer of Simeon

*And now, Lord, Your bond-servant
can go in peace,
for You have kept Your word,*

*and my eyes have witnessed Your
salvation –*

*the salvation You prepared
in the presence of all nations –*

*the Light You revealed to everyone,
the glory You have with Your people.*

Luke 11:2-4 – a prayer of Jesus

Father in heaven,
may Your Name
be kept holy among us.

Bring us into Your kingdom.

Give us bread for the day.

Forgive us
as we forgive those who
have wronged us.

Keep us from temptation.

Deliver us
from a time of hard trials.

Luke 18:13 – a prayer of a penitent

O God,
please
be merciful
to me,
a sinner.

Luke 23:34 – a prayer of Jesus

Father,
forgive them!

They don't know
what they're doing.

Luke 23:46 – a prayer of Jesus

Father,
into Your hands

I entrust
My Spirit.

John 11:41-43 – a prayer of Jesus

Father, thank You
for hearing Me.
You always listen,
but I'm saying this
so other people
can hear, too,
and believe
You sent Me.

John 12:27-28 – a prayer of Jesus

I'm troubled so deeply
I don't even know
how to express it!

Should I say, "Father,
save me from this time
of suffering?"

How can I
when it's essential
for what I came to do?

Father, glorify Your Name.

John 17:1-5 – a prayer of Jesus

Father, My time has come.
Give Your Child glory,
so Your Son can glorify You.

You have given Me authority
over all humanity, so I
can give eternal life to all
whom You gave to me.

And, this is eternal life:
To know You, the only true God,
and Jesus Christ,
Whom You have sent.

I have given You glory on earth
by finishing the work You gave Me.

Now, Father, give Me
glory in Your presence
with the glory I had with You
before the world began.

John 17:6-9 – a prayer of Jesus

*Father, I've made Your Name known
to the ones You gave Me.*

*They're from this world, but they
belong to You,
and You gave them to Me.*

They did as You asked.

*Now they know that all You have
given to Me comes from You, for
I've given them the message
You gave to Me.*

*They have accepted this word,
and they believe I came from You.
They believe You sent Me.
And so, I pray for them.*

*I'm not praying the same thing
for the world, but for the ones
You gave to Me, for they are Yours.*

John 17:10-19 – a prayer of Jesus

Holy Father, all I have belongs to You,
and all You have is mine.
The people You gave Me
have given Me glory.
I won't be in the world much longer,
but they will be in the world
as I come back to You.
Holy Father, keep them safe
by the power of Your Name –
the Name You gave to Me,
so their unity may be like Ours.

While I've been with them, I've kept them safe
by the power of Your Name – the Name You
gave to Me. I watched over them, and none,
but one, became lost, showing scripture true.
But now, Father, I'm returning to You, and I
say these things while I'm still in the world,
so they will have the same joy We have.

I have given them Your message, but the world
now hates them because they don't belong
to the world any more than I do.
I'm not asking You to take them out of the world
but to protect them from the evil one, for they
don't belong to the world any more than I do.

Let Your truth make them holy,
for Your words are truth.
I've sent them into the world as You sent me.
And so, for their sake, I dedicate Myself – I
consecrate and sanctify Myself – so they, too,
will be sanctified, consecrated, and dedicated
to the truth in You.

John 17:20-26 – a prayer of Jesus

Father, I'm not just praying for My followers now.
I'm also praying for those who believe in Me
because of their message. I pray that
all My followers will unite in the way
You, Father, are in Me, and I in You.
I pray for them to be united with Us,
so the whole world can see You sent Me.
I've given them the glory You gave to Me.
I did this, so they can become one in the way
We are One.

I Am in them. You are in Me. They are in Us.
In this way, the world can see You sent Me,
and You love them as You have loved Me.

Father, I want those You have given to Me
to be with Me – to be where I Am.

I want them to see My glory, which You gave to Me
because of Your love before the world was made!

Father, You have done what is right, and the world
didn't recognize You! But I knew You, and My followers
now know You sent me.

I have made Your Name known to them, and I will
continue to make it known, so the love You have
for Me will become part of them, and I will be in them.

Acts 1:24-25 – a prayer of Peter

Lord, You know
our thoughts
and motives.

Show us
the person
You have chosen
for this ministry.

Acts 4:29-30 – a prayer of Jesus' followers

Lord, can You hear how
they're threatening us?

Please help us to speak Your word
with courage, Lord.

Show Your power!

Bring healing!

Perform miracles for us!

Amaze everyone with the authority
found in Jesus' Name.

Acts 7:59-60 – a prayer of Stephen

Lord Jesus,
receive my spirit!

Do not hold
their acts
against me
as sin
against them.

Romans 1:8–10 – a prayer of Paul

God, I thank You
for the followers
of Jesus Christ,
whose faith now
covers the earth.

God, You are my witness
of how I've given
my whole heart
to preaching
the Good News
of Your Son.

I constantly remember
Your people in my prayers,
and I pray You will
open a way for me
to be with them.

Romans 15:5–6, 13 – a prayer of Paul

God Who gives us
endurance
and encouragement,
please give us
a spirit of unity
among ourselves.

As we follow Christ Jesus,
may we glorify You –
God and Father
of our Lord Jesus Christ –
with one heart, one mouth.

God of hope, fill us
with all joy and peace
as we trust You –
as our hope overflows
by the power
of Your Holy Spirit.

2 Corinthians 1:3–7 – a prayer of Paul

*We praise You, God and Father
of our Lord Jesus Christ – Father
of compassion and God of all
comfort, Who comforts us in all
our troubles, so we can comfort
those in trouble with the comfort
we ourselves have received from
You. For as the sufferings of Christ
comes into our lives, so also the
comfort of Christ pours upon us.*

*If we suffer distress, let it be used
for the hope of Your people.*

*If we receive comfort, let it be used
to soothe others, thereby producing
the ability to endure patiently the
distresses we all suffer.*

*And so our hope is for Your people
to stand firm, because we know
that, as they share in our trials,
they also share in our relief.*

2 Corinthians 2:14–16 – a prayer of Paul

Thank You, God!
You always lead us
in our successful
walk in Christ,
and through us,
You spray all around
the scent of knowing Him.

To You we smell like Christ!

To those being saved
and those who are
perishing –
to one we are the stench
of death, to the other
the fragrance of life.

Who is ready
for such a task?

2 Corinthians 12:8–9 – a prayer of Paul

Three times, Lord,
I've asked You to take
away this thorn
in my flesh sent
to test me.

Then I hear You say,

"My grace is
sufficient for you,
for My power
perfects your
weakness."

Ephesians 1:17-18 – a prayer of Paul

Glorious Father –
the God of our Lord Jesus Christ –
give us a spirit of wisdom
and revelation
as we come to know Christ
more and more.

Give us ever-deepening
insight, so we can truly see
the hope to which
we have been called
and the wealth of blessings
and glory we've inherited
as Your people.

Ephesians 3:14–19 – a prayer of Paul

*I'm kneeling before You, Lord –
the Father from Whom
everyone in heaven and earth
has been given Your Family Name.*

*May Your glorious riches
strengthen the inner being
of all Your people
with the power of Your Holy Spirit,
so Christ may reside
in our hearts through faith.*

*May your people be rooted
and firmly established
in Your way of love.*

*May we – and all Your people –
have the power to glimpse
how wide and long,
how high and deep
is the love of Christ.*

*Even though we can't begin
to understand,
we pray You fill us fully
with You.*

Philippians 1:9–11 – a prayer of Paul

Lord, hear my prayer:

May the love
of Your people
grow stronger
and stronger
in knowledge of You
and deeper
and deeper
with insight,
so we'll be able
to discern
what is best.

Keep us pure
and unblemished,
filled with the goodness
only Jesus Christ can give
as we await His coming
in the glory
and praise of You.

Colossians 1:14-19 – a prayer of Paul

God, fill Your people
with the knowledge of Your will,
so we'll have the spiritual wisdom
and understanding we need.

May we live lives worthy of You, Lord.

May we please You in every way:
bearing fruit in each good work,
growing in our knowledge of You,
being strengthened
though Your glorious might
with the power we need.

May we have the ability
to be patient and endure,
giving joyful thanks to You, Father,
for You have qualified us
to share in Your gifts
with all Your people
in Your kingdom of light,
for You have rescued us
from the clutches of darkness,
and You have brought us
into the kingdom of Your beloved Son
in Whom we have been redeemed –
in Whom we have been forgiven.

1 Thessalonians 1:2–3 – a prayer of Paul

God, we thank You
for Your people,
and we pray for them.

O God and Father,
may we continue
to remember
the work You
have produced in us
by our faith in You,
the labor prompted by love,
the endurance You inspired
by our hope in the Lord
Jesus Christ.

1 Thessalonians 3:9–13 – a prayer of Paul

We can't thank You enough, God,
for the joy we have
in Your presence
because of the fellowship we have
with Your people.

Night and day, we pray
most earnestly to see again
our family in the faith
and help with whatever
is lacking.

Dear God and Father,
may You and our Lord Jesus
clear the way for us
to be with Your people.

Lord, may You make
our love increase to overflowing
for each other – and everyone –
as our love pours forth for You.

May You strengthen our hearts
and help us to live
in Your presence, O God
and Father –
guiltless and consecrated
when our Lord Jesus comes
with all His holy ones.

1 Thessalonians 5:23–24, 28 – a prayer of Paul

Dear God,
sanctify us through and through –
through You –
our God of peace.

May our whole bodies,
souls, and spirits
be free of blame
at the coming
of our Lord Jesus Christ,
for You are faithful
and can do anything!

May the grace
of our Lord Jesus Christ
be with us all.

2 Thessalonians 1:11-12 – a prayer of Paul

O God, how we pray
for You to count us worthy
of Your calling!

May You fulfill
every good purpose of Yours
and every act of faith
by Your power.

May the Name of our Lord Jesus
be glorified in us,
and we in Him,
according to Your grace, O God,
and the grace of our Lord,
Jesus Christ.

2 Thessalonians 2:16–17 – a prayer of Paul

O Father God,
may You encourage
our hearts
and strengthen us
in every good word
and good deed
through our Lord
Jesus Christ, Who
loved us and,
by His grace,
gave us eternal
encouragement
and the hope
of good
forever.

2 Thessalonians 3:2–5, 16 – a prayer of Paul

Not everyone has faith, Lord!
But we pray to be delivered
from all evil and wickedness,
for You are faithful to us
and You will strengthen
and protect us from the evil one.

We place our confidence
in You, Lord,
for You are doing –
and will continue to do –
everything we need.

Direct our hearts, Lord,
into Your love
and the perseverance
of Christ.

And may You,
the Lord of peace,
give us peace
at all times
and in all ways.

May You, Lord,
be with us all.

1 Timothy 2:1-6 – a prayer of Paul

Remind us, Lord,
to make our requests –
our prayers,
intercession,
and thanksgiving –
for everyone,
including our leaders
and all those in authority,
so we may live
peaceful,
quiet,
godly,
holy lives.

Surely this pleases You,
God our Savior,
for You want everyone
to be saved
and come to know
the truth in You.

You alone are God,
and we have One
mediator between You
and other people –
the One, Christ Jesus,
Who gave Himself
as a ransom for us

and everyone.

Philemon 4, 25 – a prayer of Paul

God, may we be active
in sharing our faith
and come to a better
understanding
of the goodness
You have given us
in Christ.

May the grace
of the Lord Jesus Christ
embrace our spirit.

2 Peter 1:2 – a prayer of Peter

Lord, may grace
and peace
fill our lives
as we come
to know You,
God, and Jesus,
our Lord.

2 John 1:3 – a prayer of John

God the Father,
may Your grace, mercy,

and peace be with us
in truth and love –

O Lord and Father
of Jesus Christ.

Jude 1:1 – a prayer of Jude

Lord, may mercy,

peace,

and love

be

                lavished

upon us:

we who have been called,

we who are loved by God the Father,

we who are kept safe in Jesus Christ.

Revelation 4:8, 11 – a prayer of spiritual beings

Holy, holy, holy!
Lord, God Almighty –
worthy are You
to receive glory
and honor and power,
for You created all things,
and by Your will,
all things exist.

Revelation 5:13 – a prayer of all creatures in heaven and earth

To Him Who sits
on the heavenly throne –
and to the Lamb –

may there be blessings
      and honor
and glory
      and dominion
forever
      and ever.

Revelation 6:10 – a prayer of the martyrs

O Sovereign Lord,
holy and true –
how long will it be
before You judge
the people of this world
and bring justice
for what they have done?

Revelation 22:20-21 – a prayer of John

Marana tha—
Our Lord, come!

May the grace
of our Lord Jesus Christ
be with you all.

Amen.

Alphabetical index and identification of the ones who prayed:

[Note: *Some prayers, such as those in Psalms, may be difficult to identify, so the names given provide a general consensus.*]

Hannah – The mother of the prophet Samuel – 42
Hezekiah – A king of Judah – 58, 59
Isaiah – A major prophet – 203
Jabez – A descendant of Judah – 60
Jacob – The third patriarch, son of Isaac and Rebekah, twin brother of Esau, and husband of Rachel – 17-20
Jehoshaphat – A king of Judah – 64
Jeremiah – A major prophet in Jerusalem – 204-212
Jesus – The Christ, Messiah, Anointed One, Son of God – 228, 232, 236, 237, 242, 244-251
Jesus' followers – People from every culture – 231, 253
Job – Arabian believer in God, whose faith was tested – 74-78
John – A son of Zebedee, brother of James, and one of the twelve apostles – 273, 278
Jonah – A prophet of Israel and reluctant missionary – 219, 220
Jude – Follower of Christ – 274
Leper – Man with skin disease healed by Jesus – 229
Manoah – The father of Samson – 40
Mary – The mother of Jesus and wife of Joseph – 238, 239
Melchizedek – Mysterious high priest of Salem, who some believe to be a manifestation of Jesus – 9
Miriam – Sister of Moses and Aaron known as a prophetess – 24
Moses – A son of slaves, raised by Pharaoh's daughter, whom God chose to led the Hebrews out of captivity in Egypt and give the Ten Commandments – 21-23, 25-27, 29-37, 152
Nehemiah – Jewish exile, who helped to rebuild Jerusalem – 67, 68, 73
Parent – 234
Paul – Saul, a devout Jew, who persecuted Christians until Christ appeared to him on the road to Damascus – 255-271
Penitent – Person regretful of behavior – 243
People of Israel – God's people, the Jews – 69-72
Person who's suffering – 156-158
Peter – Fisherman also known as Simon, one of the twelve apostles, and one of Jesus' closest friends – 233, 252, 272
Rebekah – Wife of Isaac and mother of Jacob and Esau – 16
Roman officer - 230

Samson – A Nazarite and judge in Israel known for his strength and long hair – 41
Samuel – Prophet who frequently prayed for God's people but whose actual prayers were almost never recorded – 44
Sarah – Wife of Abraham and mother of their son Isaac – 14
Simeon – Elderly man who visited the Temple often and arrived when Baby Jesus was presented to the Lord - 241
Solomon – Son of King David and Bathsheba known for his wisdom and successor to the throne – 49-54
Spiritual Beings - 275
Stephen – One of the first deacons appointed by the apostles and the first Christian martyr – 254
Zechariah – A priest in Jerusalem, husband of Elizabeth, father of John the Baptist - 240

Made in the USA
Lexington, KY
23 September 2019